Barbara McClintock

AMERICAN WOMEN of ACHIEVEMENT

Barbara McClintock

MARY KITTREDGE

CHELSEA HOUSE PUBLISHERS

NEW YORK · PHILADELPHIA

Chelsea House Publishers
EDITOR-IN-CHIEF Remmel Nunn
MANAGING EDITOR Karyn Gullen Browne
COPY CHIEF Juliann Barbato
PICTURE EDITOR Adrian G. Allen
ART DIRECTOR Maria Epes
DEPUTY COPY CHIEF Mark Rifkin
ASSISTANT ART DIRECTOR Noreen Romano
MANUFACTURING MANAGER Gerald Levine
SYSTEMS MANAGER Lindsey Ottman
PRODUCTION MANAGER Joseph Romano
PRODUCTION COORDINATOR Marie Claire Cebrián

American Women of Achievement
SENIOR EDITOR Kathy Kuhtz

Staff for BARBARA McCLINTOCK
ASSOCIATE EDITOR Ellen Scordato
COPY EDITOR Brian Sookram
EDITORIAL ASSISTANT Michele Haddad
PICTURE RESEARCHER Sandy Jones
DESIGNER Diana Blume
COVER ILLUSTRATION Eileen McKeating
COVER ORNAMENT FPG International

First Printing

1 3 5 7 9 8 6 4 2

Library of Congress Cataloging-in-Publication Data

Mary Kittredge
    Barbara McClintock / by Mary Kittredge
        p. cm.—(American women of achievement)
    Summary: a biography of the geneticist who won the 1983
    Nobel Prize for her discovery that certain genes can change
    their position on the chromosomes of cells.
    ISBN 1-55546-666-4
        0-7910-0442-2 (pbk.)
    1. McClintock, Barbara, 1902–   —Juvenile literature.
2. Women geneticists—United States—Biography—Juvenile
literature. [1. McClintock, Barbara, 1902– . 2. Geneticists.]
I. Title. II. Series.
QH429.2.M38K46 1990
575. 1'092—dc20   90-1957
[B]   CIP
[92]   AC

CONTENTS

AMERICAN WOMEN OF ACHIEVEMENT

Abigail Adams
women's rights advocate

Jane Addams
social worker

Louisa May Alcott
author

Marian Anderson
singer

Susan B. Anthony
woman suffragist

Ethel Barrymore
actress

Clara Barton
*founder of the American
Red Cross*

Elizabeth Blackwell
physician

Nellie Bly
journalist

Margaret Bourke-White
photographer

Pearl Buck
author

Rachel Carson
biologist and author

Mary Cassatt
artist

Agnes de Mille
choreographer

Emily Dickinson
poet

Isadora Duncan
dancer

Amelia Earhart
aviator

Mary Baker Eddy
*founder of the Christian
Science church*

Betty Friedan
feminist

Althea Gibson
tennis champion

Emma Goldman
political activist

Helen Hayes
actress

Lillian Hellman
playwright

Katharine Hepburn
actress

Karen Horney
psychoanalyst

Anne Hutchinson
religious leader

Mahalia Jackson
gospel singer

Helen Keller
humanitarian

Jeane Kirkpatrick
diplomat

Emma Lazarus
poet

Clare Boothe Luce
author and diplomat

Barbara McClintock
biologist

Margaret Mead
anthropologist

Edna St. Vincent Millay
poet

Julia Morgan
architect

Grandma Moses
painter

Louise Nevelson
sculptor

Sandra Day O'Connor
Supreme Court justice

Georgia O'Keeffe
painter

Eleanor Roosevelt
diplomat and humanitarian

Wilma Rudolph
champion athlete

Florence Sabin
medical researcher

Beverly Sills
opera singer

Gertrude Stein
author

Gloria Steinem
feminist

Harriet Beecher Stowe
author and abolitionist

Mae West
entertainer

Edith Wharton
author

Phillis Wheatley
poet

Babe Didrikson Zaharias
champion athlete

CHELSEA HOUSE PUBLISHERS

"REMEMBER THE LADIES"

MATINA S. HORNER

Remember the Ladies." That is what Abigail Adams wrote to her husband, John, then a delegate to the Continental Congress, as the Founding Fathers met in Philadelphia to form a new nation in March of 1776. "Be more generous and favorable to them than your ancestors. Do not put such unlimited power in the hands of the Husbands. If particular care and attention is not paid to the Ladies," Abigail Adams warned, "we are determined to foment a Rebellion, and will not hold ourselves bound by any Laws in which we have no voice, or Representation."

The words of Abigail Adams, one of the earliest American advocates of women's rights, were prophetic. Because when we have not "remembered the ladies," they have, by their words and deeds, reminded us so forcefully of the omission that we cannot fail to remember them. For the history of American women is as interesting and varied as the history of our nation as a whole. American women have played an integral part in founding, settling, and building our country. Some we remember as remarkable women who—against great odds—achieved distinction in the public arena: Anne Hutchinson, who in the 17th century became a charismatic religious leader; Phillis Wheatley, an 18th-century black slave who became a poet; Susan B. Anthony, whose name is synonymous with the 19th-century women's rights movement and who led the struggle to enfranchise women; and, in our own century, Amelia Earhart, the first woman to cross the Atlantic Ocean by air.

These extraordinary women certainly merit our admiration, but other women, "common women," many of them all but forgotten, should also be recognized for their contributions to American thought and culture. Women have been community builders; they have founded schools and formed voluntary associations to help those in need; they have assumed the major responsibility for rearing children, passing on from one generation to the next the values that keep a culture alive. These and innumerable other contributions, once ignored, are now being recognized by scholars, students, and the public. It is exciting and gratifying to realize that a part of our history that was hardly acknowledged a few generations ago is now being studied and brought to light.

In recent decades, the field of women's history has grown from obscurity to a politically controversial splinter movement to academic respectability, in many cases mainstreamed into such traditional disciplines as history, economics, and psychology. Scholars of women, both female and male, have organized research centers at such prestigious institutions as Wellesley College, Stanford University, and the University of California. Other notable centers for women's studies are the Center for the American Woman and Politics at the Eagleton Institute of Politics at Rutgers University; the Henry A. Murray Research Center for the Study of Lives, at Radcliffe College; and the Women's Research and Education Institute, the research arm of the Congressional Caucus on Women's Issues. Other scholars and public figures have established archives and libraries, such as the Schlesinger Library on the History of Women in America, at Radcliffe College, and the Sophia Smith Collection, at Smith College, to collect and preserve the written and tangible legacies of women.

From the initial donation of the Women's Rights Collection in 1943, the Schlesinger Library grew to encompass vast collections documenting the manifold accomplishments of American women. Simultaneously, the women's movement in general and the academic discipline of women's studies in particular also began with a narrow definition and gradually expanded their mandate. Early causes such as woman suffrage and social reform, abolition and organized labor were joined by newer concerns such as the history of women in business and the professions and in politics and government; the study of the family; and social issues such as health policy and education.

Women, as historian Arthur M. Schlesinger, jr., once pointed out, "have constituted the most spectacular casualty of traditional history.

INTRODUCTION

They have made up at least half the human race, but you could never tell that by looking at the books historians write." The new breed of historians is remedying that omission. They have written books about immigrant women and about working-class women who struggled for survival in cities and about black women who met the challenges of life in rural areas. They are telling the stories of women who, despite the barriers of tradition and economics, became lawyers and doctors and public figures.

The women's studies movement has also led scholars to question traditional interpretations of their respective disciplines. For example, the study of war has traditionally been an exercise in military and political analysis, an examination of strategies planned and executed by men. But scholars of women's history have pointed out that wars have also been periods of tremendous change and even opportunity for women, because the very absence of men on the home front enabled them to expand their educational, economic, and professional activities and to assume leadership in their homes.

The early scholars of women's history showed a unique brand of courage in choosing to investigate new subjects and take new approaches to old ones. Often, like their subjects, they endured criticism and even ostracism by their academic colleagues. But their efforts have unquestionably been worthwhile, because with the publication of each new study and book another piece of the historical patchwork is sewn into place, revealing an increasingly comprehensive picture of the role of women in our rich and varied history.

Such books on groups of women are essential, but books that focus on the lives of individuals are equally indispensable. Biographies can be inspirational, offering their readers the example of people with vision who have looked outside themselves for their goals and have often struggled against great obstacles to achieve them. Marian Anderson, for instance, had to overcome racial bigotry in order to perfect her art and perform as a concert singer. Isadora Duncan defied the rules of classical dance to find true artistic freedom. Jane Addams had to break down society's notions of the proper role for women in order to create new social institutions, notably the settlement house. All of these women had to come to terms both with themselves and with the world in which they lived. Only then could they move ahead as pioneers in their chosen callings.

Biography can inspire not only by adulation but also by realism. It helps us to see not only the qualities in others that we hope to emulate but also, perhaps, the weaknesses that made them "human." By helping us identify with the subject on a more personal level they help us to feel that we, too, can achieve such goals. We read about Eleanor Roosevelt, for example, who occupied a unique and seemingly enviable position as the wife of the president. Yet we can sympathize with her inner dilemma: an inherently shy woman who had to force herself to live a most public life in order to use her position to benefit others. We may not be able to imagine ourselves having the immense poetic talent of Emily Dickinson, but from her story we can understand the challenges faced by a creative woman who was expected to fulfill many family responsibilities. And though few of us will ever reach the level of athletic accomplishment displayed by Wilma Rudolph or Babe Zaharias, we can still appreciate their spirit, their overwhelming will to excel.

A biography is a multifaceted lens. It is first of all a magnification, the intimate examination of one particular life. But at the same time, it is a wide-angle lens, informing us about the world in which the subject lived. We come away from reading about one life knowing more about the social, political, and economic fabric of the time. It is for this reason, perhaps, that the great New England essayist Ralph Waldo Emerson wrote, in 1841, "There is properly no history: only biography." And it is also why biography, and particularly women's biography, will continue to fascinate writers and readers alike.

Barbara McClintock

On December 10, 1983, Barbara McClintock stepped into the spotlight
when she received the Nobel Prize for medicine or physiology. The
81-year-old scientist had spent years laboring in relative obscurity,
but her ground-breaking work in genetics and visionary theories
eventually won her worldwide renown.

O N E

The Nobel Prize

On December 10, 1983, at 4:00 P.M. an 81-year-old American scientist named Barbara McClintock entered the Concert Hall in Stockholm, Sweden. Darkness had already settled over the city, for the winter days in Sweden are very short. Dozens of long black limousines lined the cobblestone street outside the entrance. They gleamed under the street lamps, and their presence testified to the importance of those gathered for the ceremony about to begin in the concert building.

Inside the ornate hall, wreaths of flowers hung from the balconies. The king and queen of Sweden had already taken their place on the stage, which was carpeted in royal blue, backed by heavy velvet draperies, and lit by chandeliers. Seated in the audience were about 1,700 guests, all formally dressed in tuxedos or evening gowns.

The time came for McClintock to make her appearance, along with the five other award winners. Like them, she was there to receive the highest honor the scientific establishment can bestow: the Nobel Prize, which she had earned for a lifetime of work on the heredity of *Zea mays*, a variety of plant popularly called maize, or Indian corn.

As the winners made their way up the center aisle to their red-velvet armchair, the trumpets in the orchestra blew a fanfare to honor them. The horns were joined by the entire orchestra as each winner mounted the stage to receive the award from the king.

Usually, music at the Nobel award ceremony is from the winners' own country. But this year marked the 150th anniversary of the birth of Alfred Nobel, an immensely wealthy Swedish businessman and the inventor of dynamite who in 1896 willed his fortune of $9 million to be given "to those who . . . conferred the greatest benefit on mankind." Each year, the interest the money had earned was divided among the winners of the award. As a tribute to Alfred Nobel, this year the orchestra played music from the four countries in which he had lived: Sweden, Russia, France, and Italy.

At last it was Barbara McClintock's turn to be honored. As the diminutive, 102-pound woman with the tanned, wrinkled face and short gray hair stood on the stage, Professor Nils Ringertz of Sweden's Karolinska Institute praised her for the "immense perseverance and skill" she had shown in her scientific work. He noted, as reported in the *New York Times* on the following day, that her work showed "how important it is that scientists are given the freedom to pursue promising lines of research without having to worry about the immediate practical implications."

Finally, King Carl Gustav of Sweden presented Barbara McClintock with a diploma honoring her as the 1983 Nobel laureate in medicine, a gold medal weighing half a pound and imprinted with the bust of Alfred Nobel, and last a check for $190,000.

The room thundered with the sound of applause, which rose and swelled until the floor of the Concert Hall seemed to shake with it. Usually sedate, the Nobel audience held nothing back as its members expressed how much they agreed with and approved of the award to McClintock. After 50 years of solitary work as a plant scientist, McClintock finally stepped into the spotlight.

At the dinner and dance at Stockholm's town hall later that evening, McClintock was given the seat of honor at the right hand of the king, leaving it only to deliver a three-minute speech about the pleasures of working alone. As she had said when her award was first announced in October of that year, she regarded her long period of lonely work not as a difficulty but as a joy and a privilege.

"It seems a little unfair," she had said at a press conference two months earlier, "to reward a person for having so much pleasure over the years." But she was greatly pleased that at long last the worldwide scientific community had recognized the value of her research.

She found the publicity that accompanied the award much less pleasant. Throughout the week of Nobel festivities in Stockholm, she was a center of attention and acclaim. Before and after every gala, dinner, and reception, reporters from news organizations all over the world pestered her for interviews, took her photograph, and asked her what she planned to do with the Nobel Prize money.

McClintock endured the attention politely but with little enthusiasm. Two years earlier, she had made her attitudes about fame and money clear when she began winning a series of prestigious science awards that led to the Nobel Prize. In 1981, when after years of being ignored she received a MacArthur Foundation award of $60,000 a year for life, a $15,000 Lasker prize for medical research, and a $50,000 award from the Wolf Foundation in Israel, she told the *New York Times*, "It's too much . . . at my age I should be allowed to do as I please and have my fun." Asked about the money the awards brought in, she said, "Those things have never been

McClintock accepts congratulations at the formal presentation of her 1981 award of $50,000 from the Wolf Foundation in Israel.

important to me. I never wanted to be bothered by possessions or to own anything."

By fun, she meant the routine she had been following for 50 years: growing corn plants, harvesting them, and studying their cells in a laboratory. She began her career in the 1920s, when science was not generally thought to be a proper sort of work for women. From the start she concentrated on the multicolored kernels of maize. Throughout the 1930s and 1940s she made impor-

tant discoveries about maize genetics. (Genetics is a branch of biology that deals with how an individual organism passes its particular traits on to its offspring.) But her findings began to meet great resistance from the majority of geneticists in the beginning of the 1950s. Her arguments and evidence were not understood or accepted by other scientists, and McClintock finally stopped trying to convince them of the value and meaning of her research.

Breeding, raising, and harvesting maize were only the first stages in McClintock's work in Cold Spring Harbor, New York; during her 40 years there she also spent long hours in her laboratory meticulously examining individual kernels and noting her observations.

Instead of abandoning her work in despair or fruitlessly trying to publish articles defending her research, she quietly worked on. She remained ensconced at a research center at Cold Spring Harbor on Long Island in New York, employed by the Carnegie Institution of Washington. For half a century, she lived alone in a tiny apartment above a garage. She had never married, did not own a car or have a telephone, and usually dressed in old dungarees, work shirts, and comfortable shoes. Saying very little about her work to others, she published reports of it only in the Carnegie Institution's annual reports, not in scientific journals.

Far from feeling deprived, though, McClintock felt this simple way of life suited her. She told a reporter in 1981 that at the age of 77, "I used to say I wanted two things," she joked, "to own an automobile and eyeglasses. Now I just want my eyeglasses."

Her daily routine was busy, complex, and almost unvarying for all those 50 years. After getting up early to exercise and eat breakfast, she went for her daily walk in the woods near her apartment. On her stroll, she paused to identify animals, plants, and birds. Next came her morning visit to the library, and by 7:00 A.M. she was usually already engrossed in reading several scientific journals. Before she left, she copied others to read later.

In autumn and winter she went next to her laboratory, to continue her work of peering through a microscope to examine the tiny structures inside the cells of corn plants. She remained at work in the lab until late at night, sometimes pausing to rest there on a cot before starting again. In the spring and summer she did the hard physical work of sowing and tending her corn plants, which grew in a garden plot about a quarter mile from the lab. In her scant spare time she socialized with a few close friends or with her niece, her niece's husband, and their son; sometimes, using the black walnuts she gathered on her morning walks in autumn, she baked cakes to give to them.

Often, however, she became so involved in her solitary work that she spoke to no one for days on end. A fellow Cold Spring Harbor scientist told one reporter that he once visited McClintock in her laboratory at 5:00 P.M. She had to apologize for croaking hoarsely to him. "Excuse me," she said, "but I have not used my vocal cords all day."

Another article recorded similar comments by her colleague Steven Dellaporta, a young biologist. "When Barbara did her experiments," Dellaporta noted, "she did everything by herself." In 1982, the 28-year-old biologist had begun studying McClintock's decades of research on the maize plant and growing more plants of his own from seeds that she provided from the last crops she had planted, in the 1960s.

On October 10, 1983, Barbara McClintock had gotten up, turned on her radio, and heard a report that changed her life. Because she had no telephone, the Karolinska Institute in Sweden was not able to call to tell her it had decided to award her the 1983 Nobel Prize in medicine. When she heard the radio report that she had won, "I knew I was going to be in for something," she told an interviewer. "I had to psych myself up. I had to think of the significance of it all. . . . I had to know what approach I would take."

In order to think about it, she had set out that morning for her daily walk. As usual, she remembered to bring a pair of tongs so that she could collect black walnuts without staining her hands. When she returned, she had decided how to deal with her far-from-usual situation. She met at once with William Udry, the administrative director of the Cold Spring Harbor laboratories, to talk things over with him.

McClintock knew that in the next few months she would be surrounded by people, by questions, and by acclaim— all of which she was unused to and none of which she wanted. Still, the award would recognize not only her personally but also the discoveries she had made and give favorable publicity to the Carnegie Institution's Cold Spring Harbor research center. She was grateful to the Carnegie Institution, and she called Cold Spring Harbor "an oasis" in one interview. "If I had been at some other place, I'm sure I would have been fired." McClintock had published little, in great contrast to the majority of researchers. Most investigators need to have their articles accepted and published in science journals—the more prestigious the journal, the better for the researcher—to prove their worth and keep their job. The struggle to publish can be competitive and time-consuming, and McClintock valued her freedom from such demands. So, in appreciation to the institute, she told Udry, "I will do what I have to do" regarding the media circus that surrounds Nobel Prize recipients.

Some of the things she had to do revealed a well-developed sense of humor as the whole world focused its attention on her. Reporters flocked to Cold Spring Harbor in the days after the Nobel announcement, trampling the lawns and hiding in the bushes in their efforts to take pictures of her. One made it all the way into her laboratory, but just as he was about to snap a photograph of McClintock she pulled a bag over her head. Those who telephoned her lab received a less friendly reception. One of her colleagues at Cold Spring Harbor told of how McClintock, irritated by the constant interruptions from the ringing telephone in her office, picked up the receiver, waved it in the air for a few moments, then set it down again with a click.

Her other responses, however, were more hospitable: Hours after the Nobel award had been announced, she held a press conference so that reporters would have a chance to ask questions and write their stories. One journalist asked, "What do you think of big to-dos like this, with all the attention that's being heaped on you?" McClintock answered dryly, "You put up with it." She did so graciously. She allowed pictures to be taken of herself and her corn plants. Holding an ear of corn in hands bent with arthritis, the tiny, bespectacled woman with the short-cropped hair and wrinkled face appeared to be rather proud of her cherished, brightly colored maize.

Still, it was clear she was not accustomed to such attention. When reporters at the press conference asked her how she felt about all the interest she and her corn were suddenly getting, she said in a voice nearly as quiet as a whisper: "You don't need the public recognition." When asked how she felt about how long it had taken for her work to be deemed important and correct, she replied, "If you know you're right, you don't care. You know that sooner or later, it will come out in the wash."

After the questions had been answered, the photographs taken, and the interviews given, the 81-year-old Nobel Prize–winning scientist retreated to her experiments and rarely appeared in public again until it was time for the award ceremonies in Stockholm. When they were complete, she returned alone to Cold Spring Harbor and the things she had loved most for more than 50 years: her corn plants, her ongoing research, and her solitude.

On the arm of King Carl Gustav XVI of Sweden, McClintock makes her way through the Concert Hall in Stockholm, Sweden. More comfortable in blue jeans and a simple crew neck, McClintock found the pomp and pageantry of the Nobel award ceremony quite a contrast to her usual surroundings.

In 1923, McClintock received her baccalaureate degree from Cornell University, where she majored in botany. Two years later she acquired a master's degree, and in 1927 she earned a Ph.D., also in botany.

T W O

An Unconventional Upbringing

Barbara McClintock was born in Hartford, Connecticut, on June 16, 1902, the third daughter of Thomas Henry McClintock and Sara Handy McClintock. Sara Handy had been born on January 22, 1875, to Sara Watson Rider and Benjamin Franklin Handy. Both sides of her Massachusetts family were socially important and wealthy, and both her parents were descended from colonists who had come to America on the *Mayflower*. Thomas McClintock was born in 1876 in Natick, a small town near Boston, Massachusetts. His parents had immigrated to New England from the British Isles.

Sara's mother died when she was an infant, so her father, a minister of the Congregational church, sent her to California to be raised by an aunt and uncle who had gone there in the 1880s to prospect for gold. In that rough-and-ready gold-mining territory, prospectors still set out alone with their pack-laden mules to pan the rivers or dig with shovels and pickaxes. Some struck it rich, returning with bags full of shining nuggets. Others did not return at all, vanishing instead in the vast, unforgiving California wilderness.

Sara Handy's independent forebears no doubt helped form her own strong personality, aspects of which she would later pass on to her own daughter. But when Sara became a young woman she realized that conditions in the California mining towns were too primitive for her; she was interested in music and the arts, not the hard life of a miner's wife. So she embarked on the long cross-country train trip alone, to return to the more refined atmosphere of her father's home in Massachusetts. There she took music and painting lessons, had an active social life, and met a young medical student named Thomas McClintock.

McClintock was attractive and intel-

Sara Handy and Thomas Henry McClintock married despite the opposition of Sara's socially prominent father, the Reverend Benjamin Handy. Sara was a gifted pianist and artistically inclined; Thomas was a physician.

ligent, but he had little money and not much hope of earning any soon; all he did have went to pay his tuition at the Boston University School of Medicine. What was worse, in the opinion of Sara's father, was that McClintock's immigrant family was as obscure as Sara Handy's was prominent. The Reverend Benjamin Handy greatly disapproved of the young man, who could not give his daughter the comfortable home or high social standing she had always enjoyed. If she married Thomas McClintock, Sara's father told her angrily, he would cut her off without a penny—and she knew he meant what he said.

But Sara Handy loved Thomas McClintock and married him anyway, in 1898, paying his school tuition with money of her own. They lived for a time in Maine, New Hampshire, and the city of Hartford, Connecticut, before finally settling in Brooklyn, New York, where McClintock worked for Standard Oil as a physician to crew members of tankers that docked at the busy Brooklyn shipyard. There they raised four children: Marjorie, born in late 1898; Mignon, born in 1900; Barbara; and Malcolm Rider, born in 1905 and known as Tom.

Even as an infant, Barbara McClintock was unusually thoughtful, independent, and curious. Her biographer, Evelyn Fox Keller, author of a book on McClintock's life and work called *A Feeling for the Organism*, wrote that the McClintocks at first meant to call the infant Eleanor, a pretty and "feminine" name, but when they saw how vigorous and strong willed she was they decided that the name Barbara was more suited to her. "My mother used to put a pillow on the floor and give me one toy and leave me there," McClintock told Keller. "She said I didn't cry."

The McClintock household was run on rather unusual lines. The McClintocks encouraged all their children to be independent and to develop wide-ranging interests. Dr. McClintock even forbade their teachers to give them homework, saying that when they were not in school they should be finding out about other things. Going to school at all, in fact, was not high on the list of the McClintocks' priorities for their offspring; when Barbara grew interested in ice-skating, they bought her a fine pair of skates and allowed her to stay away from school on good ice-skating days. That she should be healthy and happy was more important to her parents than that she followed rules.

One thing they did not particularly want her to do, however, was attend college. In spite of her irregular attendance, she did so well in all her classes that by age 16 she had finished high school. She was determined to continue her education. But the McClintocks were not convinced that a college education was desirable for a young woman; at that time, in 1918, women were expected to become good wives and mothers, not career women or intellectuals. Very few jobs were open to women, so most had to marry and depend on their husband's income.

Back row: *Thomas and Sara McClintock.* Front row, left to right: *Barbara, Mignon, Marjorie, and Tom. Sara and Thomas McClintock encouraged their four children to pursue their interests as they wished. Thomas instructed the children's teachers not to assign them homework so their afternoons would be free.*

Sara McClintock was particularly worried that if Barbara went to college, she would become better educated than the young men her age, ensuring a hard life without a husband.

Another obstacle in the way of Barbara's attending college was money. The family was never wealthy, and during the years of World War I (1914–18), their financial situation worsened. Dr. McClintock was a member of the National Guard and had been sent to Europe to care for the wounded U.S. troops there. While he was gone, Sara McClintock had to give music lessons to meet the family budget, and finding money to pay for Barbara's college tuition was impossible.

For six months after Barbara graduated from high school, she worked in an employment agency to help support her family. Although attending college seemed like a distant dream, Barbara was determined to further her education. After working all day interviewing job applicants at the agency, she spent evenings and weekends in the library, trying to educate herself independently.

When her father returned from Europe in the summer of 1918, he saw her dedication to learning. Her resolution convinced him that she should have the opportunity for which she longed. He was impressed, too, that she had even found a solution to her lack of money: She explained that she would attend Cornell University's College of Agriculture because the tuition there was free. At last Dr. McClintock persuaded his wife that Barbara should be allowed to leave their home in Brooklyn and move to Ithaca, New York, to attend Cornell.

Determined to make the most of this chance, McClintock took the 175-mile train trip to Ithaca, a very different environment from the bustle of Brooklyn, even though the streets of Brooklyn were not as congested as they would become and small farms still dotted the outer reaches of the borough. Cornell was deep in the countryside, surrounded by farms and wilderness. The university was located on Lake Cayuga, one of the five Finger Lakes in western New York. Freezing winds blew across the water, making winters in Ithaca particularly harsh. Rolling hills cut by deep gorges formed a spectacular background for the sprawling campus. The terrain was so lovely and wild that the first *Tarzan* movies had been filmed there. Despite the university's isolation, student life there was filled with activity.

McClintock was assigned a room in the women's dormitory and plunged at once into all the college had to offer. Socially and scholastically, she was an immediate success. Always lively and outgoing, she quickly made friends and became so popular that she was elected president of the women's freshman class. She often went out on dates with the young men at the college and formed close friendships with several of them. Filled with enthusiasm, she signed up for many more courses than she could complete. If the classes bored her, she quickly dropped the course, but she earned high marks in ones that interested her. In every way—or so it seemed at first—Cornell was just perfect for Barbara McClintock.

Gradually, however, McClintock came to see that some parts of college life did not suit her. As a freshman, she was delighted by an invitation to join a sorority, until she learned that many of her close friends, who were Jewish, had not been offered the opportunity to join. The discovery appalled her. "I just couldn't stand that kind of discrimination," she said. "It was so shocking that I never really got over it." After thinking it over, she turned the sorority invitation down.

In the matter of clothing and hairstyles she also chose an original course. At the beginning of the 1920s, most women kept both their hair and their dresses long. In cities such as New York and Chicago, chic and stylish young women called flappers had began to shock society by bobbing their hair (cutting it short) and raising their hemlines drastically. But McClintock was certainly not a flapper and had little interest in fashion. Her unconventionality had a different source. She had been raised by her strong-minded parents to think for herself and to dress in ways that were practical. Her mother had even had a tailor sew trousers for Barbara to wear under her skirts so that as a child she could climb trees and play games just as the boys did. Reflecting on her childhood behavior, McClintock told her biographer, Keller, "I found that . . . because it was not the standard conduct, [doing as I liked] might cause me great pain, but I would take the consequences for the sake of an activity that I knew would give me great pleasure."

As an energetic college student, she found long hair was hot, messy, and difficult to take care of, so she had her hair cut short—a daring move in the 1920s that caused considerable comment among her fellow students. Her parents had always encouraged her to do as she liked as a child, and as a college student she blithely disregarded comments about her appearance. To her, short hair made good sense, so she kept it; she never minded what other people thought. By her third year at

Barbara attended grammar school at P.S. 139 in Brooklyn, New York. A photograph of her first-grade class shows her at the far right in the front row; on the blackboard in the back of the room her name appears on the right with that of the four other girls who made the honor roll.

A snapshot taken at the McClintocks' home in Brooklyn reveals Barbara relaxing while on vacation from school. Barbara greatly enjoyed her college years at Cornell, where she was a popular member of her class.

college, she also began to narrow down her academic interests and to think about which subjects she would study seriously. She had always been fascinated by the way things worked. Her curiosity dated from her earliest childhood, when on visits to a favorite uncle she would watch him repair his truck. At the age of five, she had asked her father for a set of tools and been disappointed when the tools he gave her were toys. "I wanted *real* tools," she said.

She indulged her interest in the workings of all kinds of things during her first two years at Cornell, delving into a number of different subjects, including music and geology, among others. But during her junior year of college, she took a course in genetics and found the subject more exciting than any other she had studied. "I just knew I had to go on," she said about genetics.

The plant-breeding department where genetics was studied at Cornell did not accept women students, however. (At the time, there were no laws forbidding discrimination in the education of women.) So after gaining her baccalaureate degree in 1923, McClintock joined the botany (plant science) department as a graduate student, concentrating on plant cytology (the study of cells). Continuing her independent ways, she decided that skirts inhibited her movement while working in the fields, so she wore below-the-knee trousers called knickers. In addition, she played the banjo in a jazz band that performed for student dances. But these were minor

aspects of her life, for her studies remained her absorbing interest.

During the next four years, she became deeply immersed in learning about the genetics of a single plant: maize. Ears of maize bore kernels in a variety of colors, unlike more common varieties of corn. By studying the color patterns of kernels on the cobs and relating the patterns to the inner structures of the maize plants' cells, she began to recognize how differences in the cells (visible under the microscope) corresponded to differences in the color patterns of the kernels.

By the late 20th century, it was well known that living things pass their characteristics, called traits, to their offspring through their genes— inherited bits of information that direct the development of a new organism. The genes are located inside cells on strandlike structures called chromosomes and are arranged in linear order, much like—but not exactly like— beads on a string. A new organism receives half of its genes from its mother and half from its father; this is why, for instance, a blue-eyed, brown-haired mother and a brown-eyed, red-haired father may have a blue-eyed, red-haired child. Some genes are dominant and will influence the development of the organism whenever they are present; others are recessive and will only affect an organism if inherited from both parents. It is now also known that parts of genes can move around on chromosomes and that they operate or do not operate according to regulating systems working in the cells.

To scientists of the 1920s, however, this was not all familiar information. The rules that govern how genes are passed to offspring and which ones will be expressed (affect the offspring's appearance) were first described by an Austrian scientist-monk named Gregor Mendel (1822–84) in 1866, but his work was ignored by scientists of his time. Not until 1900 was his theory, called the theory of Mendelian inheritance, rediscovered and confirmed by three scientists: Hugo de Vries, Karl Correns, and Erich von Tschermak. In 1920, researchers firmly believed that genes were fixed in their positions on the chromosomes; the idea that they might move around had not even been conceived. Other theories in genetics were not so well established, and debates still raged about exactly what a gene was. In fact, to Barbara McClintock and other scientists of her time the whole subject of genetics was an exciting, nearly unexplored frontier in which almost everything of importance still remained to be discovered.

While in graduate school, without ever announcing that she would pursue science as a career, Barbara McClintock developed into a scientist. As a graduate student, she became particularly adept in the delicate technique of preparing cells for viewing under a microscope: sectioning (thin slicing), fixing (preserving), and staining (coloring) the delicate specimens so their inner structures could be clearly seen. In addition, she had great powers of concentration and was able to forget herself and everything around her as she gazed intently for hours at corn chromosomes.

As a result, in her first year as a graduate student, McClintock achieved her first scientific discovery. Corn cells were known to contain 10 different chromosomes, but no one could tell them apart. By noting differences in the chromosomes' relative length, patterns of staining, and the occurrence of knobs in characteristic positions, McClintock quickly learned to distinguish chromosomes from one another just by looking at them—accomplishing with ease what had until that time seemed impossible.

Her ability to master difficult laboratory skills and to concentrate intensely on observing cells through the microscope was matched by a capacity for—and willingness to perform—difficult physical work. This too was a requirement for the kind of science she was pursuing, for in order to perform her experiments she could not use randomly selected maize plants. Instead, she had to raise the plants herself from seeds whose origin she knew, to keep track of which offspring inherited which traits from which parent plants. So in the spring she planted the seeds; during the hot summers she watered, weeded, and cultivated them. When the dark brown tassels appeared at the tops of the maize plants and silky golden strands lower on the stalks showed where the ears of maize would grow, the next part of her work began.

Corn kernels—the seeds of corn plants—form after pollen from the brown tassels (the male part) of one plant reaches the silky strands extend-

Arthur Sherburne, an instructor in chemistry at Cornell and a friend of McClintock's, poses next to his laboratory equipment. McClintock enthusiastically enrolled in a wide range of science courses but became fascinated by the field of genetics, which was then a fairly new science in which much remained to be discovered.

ing from the young cob (a plant's female part) on another plant. Normally, pollen is carried from one plant to another by wind or insects. For her experiments, however, McClintock had to control which tassels pollinated which cobs. So she carried pollen by hand from the tassels of some plants to the silk strands of others, keeping a careful written record of this process, which is called cross-pollinization.

In the autumn, when the cobs had matured into ears of corn, McClintock harvested the plants to study how their genes produced the patterns of color in the corn kernels. For all this labor McClintock's early life had prepared her well, for while other young women of the time might think farming was too hot, dirty, and undignified an occupation for them, McClintock accepted it as a matter of course. Her parents had

A group of researchers examine corn in the plant-breeding garden at Cornell, around 1919. The paper bags atop the cornstalks prevented the pollen of one plant from being blown by the wind and randomly fertilizing other plants. McClintock and her fellow students spent hours affixing such bags to the plants they studied, then removing them and cross-fertilizing carefully selected plants by hand. Such painstaking attention was necessary to ensure that they knew exactly which parent plants had contributed genetic material to the individual ones they analyzed.

Students work in a plant-breeding class at Cornell. McClintock wanted to enroll in the plant-breeding department for her graduate work, but that department accepted only men.

raised her to pursue her interests, not reject them as unsuitable for a woman. Like skating on school days, like wearing practical, comfortable short hair and pants, raising corn seemed a perfectly normal activity to Barbara McClintock—an activity that gave her pleasure. It was, after all, necessary to pursuing her interest in plant genetics—an interest that by 1923, when McClintock was 21, had already become the central focus of her life.

Standing, left to right: *Charles Burnham, Marcus Rhoades, Rollins Emerson, and Barbara McClintock. (Each man in the back row has a bundle of paper bags for covering corn tassels tucked into his belt.) Kneeling with dog: George Beadle. Cornell was at the forefront of maize genetics research when this picture was taken in 1929. Two of the five scientists pictured later won a Nobel Prize: George Beadle in 1958 and McClintock in 1983.*

THREE

Cornell Years

When Barbara McClintock decided to remain at Cornell and work toward her master's degree and doctorate, she made maize genetics the focus of her studies. Adept at preparing plant cells for observation through the microscope and identifying the threadlike chromosomes in them, she eagerly looked forward to learning more of the secrets of heredity.

Knowing as much as possible about how plants pass on their traits—color, shape, size, and so on—to their offspring is important for two main reasons: First, such knowledge about how specific plants pass on traits can be applied to plants in general and eventually tells scientists how all kinds of organisms pass on traits—that is, it increases their knowledge of genetics. But this information has practical use as well: Identifying the chromosomes that control specific traits is important to breeders who try to make plants

more useful to humans. Knowing which chromosomes govern resistance to disease helps in developing disease-resistant corn; to develop corn that can grow in dry areas of the world, scientists find it useful to know which chromosomes allow the plant to live without much water. Once the genetic makeup of a plant is understood—for example, knowing whether the desired trait is carried by a dominant or recessive gene is crucial in breeding—growers can concentrate on ensuring that the corn plants they raise will carry the chromosome that bears the desirable gene, and they can produce such plants in large numbers.

McClintock did not focus on the practical applications of corn genetics. For her the kernels of maize were fascinating windows into the way nature operated and particularly how genetics operated. Others shared her deep fascination with the process of heredity.

During the years from 1923 to 1927, when Barbara McClintock was earning her master's degree and then her Ph.D. at Cornell, the university was a center for the advanced study of maize genetics. The dean of the graduate school and chairman of the plant-breeding department was Rollins Emerson, an important, well-known maize geneticist who was held in great esteem not only for his own work on maize but also for his teaching ability. His reputation attracted talented students from all over the country to his laboratory at Cornell.

Among those students were Marcus M. Rhoades and George W. Beadle, both of whom were interested in maize genetics and who became lifelong friends of McClintock's. During their summers at Cornell the three would picnic at the cornfield where the plants for experiments were being grown, eagerly discussing their work and happily munching their sandwiches amid their research subjects.

In later years all three went on to earn scientific renown: Rhoades rose to prominence for his work in plant genetics, and Beadle shared the 1958 Nobel Prize in physiology for his work on enzymes (substances that speed chemical reactions in cells). But at the time, fame was far from the young scientists' minds; it was science itself, learning for its own sake, that excited them all.

McClintock's Cornell colleagues expressed enthusiastic interest in and support for her ideas. They were people with whom she could discuss her experiments in depth and whose work she was able to support and learn from in return. Both Rhoades and Beadle as well as Rollins Emerson knew from the beginning of their association with McClintock that she was as talented and brilliant as they were. That she was a woman had no bearing on their respect for her; not until later in her career did her gender begin putting any serious obstacles in her way. Interestingly, the proportion of all trained scientists who were women had reached a peak in 1920. By 1970, the proportion was less than half what it had been 50 years before. At the time McClintock was a graduate student, her gender made her unusual but certainly not a freak; she was by no means the only woman at Cornell who studied science.

Half a century later Keller met Marcus Rhoades to interview him about McClintock. "She was something special," Rhoades said. "I've known a lot of famous scientists, but the only one I thought really was a genius was McClintock." George Beadle, also interviewed by Keller, agreed. "She was so good!" Beadle exclaimed.

When McClintock completed her Ph.D. in 1927, she was appointed an instructor at Cornell. By that time she had strictly narrowed down her range of activities until only her scientific work remained. She no longer played banjo in the jazz group and had given up dating. No deep resentment of men or marriage in general motivated her withdrawal; she merely found she had no desire to pursue them for herself. Compared to her all-consuming interest in science, romantic entanglements held little attraction for her. After her encounter with the anti-Semitic sorority she flatly refused to join any organizations, including Sigma Delta Epsilon, a group for women graduate students in science. Her life had become that of a professional scientist and revolved around the cornfield, the classrooms, and the laboratories at Cornell.

McClintock was absolutely happy with her situation, for she was doing exactly what she wanted to do. Between 1929 and 1931, McClintock published nine papers on the relationship between traits expressed by individual plants and the microscopic appearance of chromosomes controlling the traits. From identifying the 10 chromosomes of the corn plant, she had progressed in her research to more detailed study of the chromosomes themselves. Her next field of inquiry was devoted to locating specific genes on chromosomes. She was particularly interested in linked genes, separate genes located on the same chromosome that usually pass together from the parent plant to its offspring. (In human beings an example of linked genes includes those that produce red hair and freckles: The traits are carried by separate genes but are very frequently inherited together.) Yet linked genes do not always behave as if they were a single gene; sometimes they become separated. An investigation of the separation of linked genes led to McClintock's first public scientific triumph.

In 1929, another female student joined Cornell's botany department: Harriet Creighton, a 20-year-old gradu-

ate teaching assistant. She had received her baccalaureate degree from Wellesley College the previous spring and was prepared to lead introductory classes for undergraduates and grade their papers, but she had not yet decided what she herself would study when she met Barbara McClintock. By the end of the day that the two women met, McClintock had arranged Creighton's entire program of study; by the end of that year, she had involved Creighton in a maize genetics experiment that brought them both to the forefront of the scientific world.

Study of the genetic makeup of individuals reveals that one set of genes comes from each parent. Almost all cells in living things have a full complement of genes, and if two of these cells joined, the offspring would have twice the standard number of chromosomes; their offspring would have four times the standard number, and so on. This problem does not arise because the cells that join together in reproduction, called gametes, are different. Gametes are formed by a process called meiosis, in which they split apart twice and each cell winds up with half the usual number of chromosomes. The joining of two such cells, one from each parent, gives rise to a zygote with the proper number of genetic elements, which develops into an individual.

Briefly, the experiment McClintock gave Creighton to perform was to demonstrate that when corn cells undergo meiosis, some of their chromosomes exchange genetic information. Two chromosomes may break, intertwine, and rejoin in a new combination. This phenomenon explains how linked genes can sometimes become separated. The gene for red hair may be on part of a chromosome that breaks off and joins with another part of a chromosome that does not have the gene for freckles, for instance. This chromosome is then passed on to one offspring. Most geneticists believed that this exchange, called crossing-over, occurred, but no one had yet proved it.

At the time, McClintock did not know that another scientist, a German researcher named Curt Stern, had undertaken almost the same project at the same time but was looking for the process in *Drosophila*, or fruit flies, instead of corn. Fruit flies reproduce much more quickly than corn does, so Stern had a head start almost at once, for he could observe the results of his breeding experiments in many generations of flies in the time in which it took McClintock and Creighton to grow and observe one crop.

Coincidentally, however, in the spring of 1931 a renowned visitor arrived at Cornell to give a series of lectures. Thomas Hunt Morgan's fame in the world of genetics was unparalleled because of his pioneering studies of inheritance in fruit flies. When he learned of McClintock and Creighton's research he encouraged them to prepare an article about their work immediately.

Both women had thought it was too early to do so and felt that they ought to have more results before trying to publish an article. But the urging of such a respected authority in their field

emboldened them, and they sent a report on their work with the data they had accumulated to the *Proceedings of the National Academy of Sciences*, which published their article in August 1931. As a result, McClintock and Creighton were credited with being the first to prove that chromosome exchange occurred during meiosis, months before Stern released his fruit fly data.

The next year, Creighton and McClintock prepared to present their findings on crossing-over before a live audience: the more than 500 geneticists from around the world who had journeyed to Ithaca to attend the Sixth International Congress of Genetics. The two women carefully prepared their report on crossing-over, which was greeted with great interest. In addition, McClintock's work was referred to in the presentations of at least five other scientists, and she gave another presentation of her own, on a separate area of chromosome research. The enthusiasm with which her work was received marked McClintock's acceptance as a full-fledged member of the world's community of professional scientists.

One of McClintock's personal triumphs resulted from the congress but did not occur at the meeting itself. Instead, it happened afterward, on a ship carrying some of the scientists back to Europe—a ship upon which McClintock herself was not even present. McClintock was delighted when she learned that one of the scientists on his way home discovered that

Gemma Jackson (left) received her Ph.D. from Cornell in 1925 and was a good friend of McClintock's. A number of women did graduate work at the university, among them Harriet Creighton, who arrived at Cornell in 1929 and soon became McClintock's co-worker. Together they performed ground-breaking genetics research.

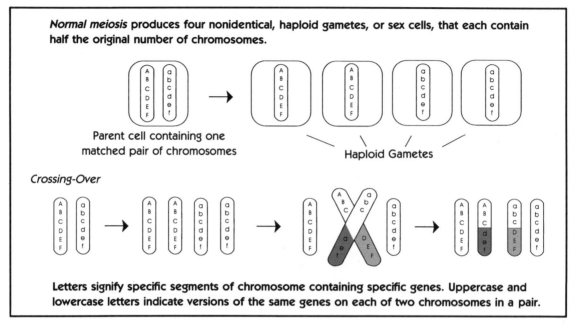

Normal meiosis produces four nonidentical, haploid gametes, or sex cells, that each contain half the original number of chromosomes.

Parent cell containing one matched pair of chromosomes

Haploid Gametes

Crossing-Over

Letters signify specific segments of chromosome containing specific genes. Uppercase and lowercase letters indicate versions of the same genes on each of two chromosomes in a pair.

A diagram schematically depicts meiosis and crossing-over. When McClintock and Creighton had their paper on the process published in 1931, they became the first scientists to prove that the phenomenon took place.

Barbara McClintock's parents were also among the passengers, heading for a European vacation. When the scientist told the McClintocks what a great success their daughter was at the congress and about the importance of the work she and Creighton had done, they were finally at ease over the life their daughter had chosen for herself. At last they were confident that letting Barbara attend college and do exactly as she wished had been the right decision after all.

At about the same time, however, McClintock began facing tough decisions of her own. As a scientist she was becoming important, respected, and well known all over the world. But at Cornell she was not promoted from her low-level job as an instructor. The reason was that she was a woman. Although her gender meant little to her peers in science, it was a heavy strike against her in the eyes of college administrators.

Women, in those days, were simply not given high-level teaching positions. Such jobs were reserved for men. The area of professional science was rather new, and some administrators felt that the prestige of the field would be harmed if women attained positions of authority at universities. Also, women were expected to marry and raise children—activities that did not combine well with scientific research. Although many women in the 1920s were scientifically trained, astonishingly few were professors. Some married other scientists and worked in their husband's laboratory; some remained as low-level instructors at coeducational schools or joined the faculty at a women's college, where they could earn great respect as teachers and advance through the hierarchy to positions of importance. Creighton eventually chose this course, but like others who did, she dropped out of the mainstream of research. The concept of equal employment rights for women was decades off; women did not even have the right to vote until 1928. Denied advancement at her alma mater, McClintock unhappily left Cornell. She had just been awarded a fellowship from the National Research Council, and for the next two years she supported herself with it while continuing her maize experiments at the University of Missouri, Pasadena's California Institute of Technology, and at Cornell, where her corn plants still grew.

At the University of Missouri she worked with a former Cornell colleague named Lewis Stadler. He was studying the effects of X rays on corn chromosomes and invited McClintock to join in the research. It was her task to identify under the microscope the specific X-ray-induced changes in chromosomes that caused obvious abnormalities in the X-ray-exposed corn plants that were passed on to later generations. Such inherited changes are called mutations and included dramatic, radical changes in the kernels' color and shape.

McClintock observed a great number of new changes in the chromosomes of such plants and kept thinking about them during the next winter as she received reports of other scientists' work on X-ray-exposed corn. Based on her observation of the Stadler plants and her experience with maize, she theorized that chromosomes exposed to X rays might be forming rings: breaking and then growing back together in ring shapes. She wrote to Stadler and scientists in Berkeley, California, who were also working on the idea, about her ring chromosome theory.

By the following year, Stadler's team of scientists at Missouri were calling the plants McClintock had studied ring chromosome plants, although no one had ever seen a ring chromosome. The idea McClintock had come up with made so much good sense that her colleagues had adopted it at once without any microscopic evidence.

Finally, though, it was time to prove the idea by actually looking for the ring chromosomes through the microscope. "Then," McClintock recalled, "I got scared. When the first plant was opened . . . my hand was actually shaking. I took it right back to the lab, and . . . it had rings." The next winter the Berkeley scientists invited her to look at their plant cells, too. There under the microscope again were the ring chromosomes she had predicted must be forming.

The 24 months of McClintock's work funded by the National Research Council produced many discoveries as her investigations and understanding of chromosomes became more complex. In addition to the formation of ring chromosomes, she observed three other main kinds of chromosomal abnormalities in Stadler's corn cells: deletions (information dropped from a chromosome), inversions (information that appears backward on the chromosome), and translocations (information moved from one spot to another on the chromosome).

At Cal Tech she discovered the "nucleolar organizing region," a spot in the cell's center whose precise purpose in the cell's function is not completely known to this day. And at Cornell, where she made her "home base" with a physician friend, Dr. Esther Parker, she continued growing the generations of corn plants that were the basis for her own work. Even though Cornell had not been willing to promote her, she was still on friendly terms with the university and members of her old de-

A 1929 photograph includes the members of the Department of Plant Breeding, graduate students in that program, and geneticists working in other departments at Cornell. McClintock (front row, center, seated) held the post of instructor at Cornell at the time.

The agriculture building at the University of Missouri housed a number of important researchers. During the summer of 1931, McClintock worked at the university with Lewis Stadler investigating the mutations that developed in cells irradiated with X rays. Her work there led to her discovery of ring chromosomes.

partment and was able to use laboratory space and borrow equipment there. Traveling between Ithaca, Missouri, and the California Institute of Technology in her own Model A Ford Roadster, completely free and utterly absorbed by her research, McClintock had until then overcome obstacles simply by going around them. Her mind was focused entirely on her work; Keller reports that McClintock told her a story about driving the Model A on a highway at a time when automobile accidents were often being reported in the news: "My only concern," McClintock said, "was that if I were killed I'd never get the answer to that [scientific] problem!"

But in 1932, even as McClintock was busily conducting her experiments and organizing her life, other lives were being torn apart. Although she did not yet realize it, the world of science was not the only world that affected her: In Germany the Nazi movement grew stronger, and unrest brewed in Europe. In 1933, McClintock was startled to confront the beginnings of Hitler's madness for herself: suddenly, without warning, and alone.

The 1930s were a difficult time for McClintock as she struggled to find a place to settle in and pursue her research. A snapshot taken during that decade shows her resting for a moment on a trip through California and Arizona.

FOUR

Finding a Home

In 1933, much of the scientific world was occupied with the new discoveries being made in the field of genetics. But the eyes of world politicians were turning uneasily toward Germany, for in January of that year Adolf Hitler, the fanatically anti-Jewish, anti-Communist, and power-hungry leader of the Nazi, or National Socialist, party, was appointed chancellor of the German government and quickly acquired what amounted to dictatorial powers.

The enormous support Hitler had from a wide range of German people, along with his well-known virulent hatred for minorities and his determination to achieve world power, made statesmen and leaders extremely apprehensive about what would happen next in Germany under his rule. What ensued—vicious persecution of Jews and other minorities, the eventual slaughter of 6 million Jews in concen-

tration camps, and World War II—was a tragedy of immense proportions. But in 1933, few outside Germany saw the horror approaching.

Barbara McClintock, who later described herself as rather politically naive, certainly did not realize what was going on in Germany. When her National Research Council grant ended at the close of 1932, Thomas Hunt Morgan, Lewis Stadler, and Rollins Emerson supported her for a Guggenheim Fellowship. Her research was world renowned and her backers' credentials were impeccable, ensuring her a grant. The Guggenheim Foundation funded her travel to Berlin, where she was to work with geneticist Richard Goldschmidt. McClintock accepted the prestigious award, although the scientist she had hoped to work with, Curt Stern, had left Germany. Had she known the precise circumstances that

47

forced Stern, who was Jewish, to flee his homeland, she might have reconsidered her journey. (Goldschmidt was Jewish also, but his distinguished position as director of the Kaiser Wilhelm Institute protected him in the early years of Nazi rule.) Blithely unaware of Hitler's persecutions, as were most Americans, McClintock set off for Germany, in happy anticipation of the experiments she would perform with the well-known, controversial Goldschmidt. She did not realize that Germany itself was being transformed into an experiment in terror. When she arrived, however, she confronted the truth almost at once, and the situation shocked her deeply.

Memoirs of Berlin residents reveal the atmosphere prevailing in the capital and throughout the country during the early 1930s. Martha Dodd, daughter of the United States ambassador to Germany at the time, described the dreadful environment in 1933 in her book *Through Embassy Eyes*: "Military camps, air-fields, concentration camps ... were sprouting up all over the country ... huge transport trucks with war material [were on the move]." Clearly, Germany was preparing for war.

At the same time, anxiety in Germany among those who were not Nazis was rising—for good reason. Hitler's persecutions grew more intense day by day. In February 1933, Hitler had seized dictatorial power by blaming a fire in the Reichstag building on Communists and succeeded in having their party banned. Anyone accused of Commu-

nist leanings was subject to arrest. Those Jews who were able to, such as Curt Stern, had fled the country, for Hitler's virulent anti-Semitism was well known and soon became national policy; but those without money to leave lived in fear for their life, and many had already been arrested. Hitler's special police, the SS and the Gestapo, sent millions to suffer and die in concentration camps. McClintock found herself surrounded by an oppressive atmosphere of terror.

"Cars had driven up in the middle of the night," Dodd wrote. "SS men had jumped out and in a moment had come down from a house or an apartment, with a man or woman who was never seen again." Sometimes even Dodd's well-connected friends, people whose importance should have protected them, were seized. No one, it seemed, was safe.

Unable to work in such an atmosphere and remembering her many Jewish friends at home, McClintock suffered miserably for a few months in Berlin. Deeply disturbed, she fled back to Cornell in December 1933, only to find that job opportunities in scientific research, especially but not only for women, had dried up. Little money was available to pay for scientific work, for the United States was suffering from the Great Depression, a worldwide economic crisis that by 1933 had thrown 16 million Americans (one-third of the nation's labor force) out of work.

For two years, McClintock's old friend and teacher Rollins Emerson managed to obtain funding for her

Nazi soldiers arrest Jewish factory workers in Germany. Although McClintock won a prestigious fellowship from the Guggenheim Foundation to study in Berlin in 1933, she was so horrified and repelled by Nazi oppression in Germany that she fled back to Cornell after only a few months there.

work, supposedly as his assistant in his lab at Cornell, through a Rockefeller Foundation grant with which he paid her salary.

Actually, she was pursuing her own research, not assisting Emerson, and everyone who was involved in genetics knew it—a state of affairs that McClintock found highly unpleasant. Although job opportunities were severely limited, she was by then quite a renowned scientist; if she had been a

man, no such arrangement would have been necessary in order for her to work, even in those economic times. Her old colleagues Rhoades and Beadle were supported with grants as she was, but their grants were their own, and they could endure hard times by looking forward to obtaining secure faculty research positions; McClintock could not.

Although the position with Emerson at Cornell did help her out in the short

Rollins Emerson, a highly esteemed maize geneticist and chairman of the plant-breeding department at Cornell, greatly respected McClintock and supported her throughout her early career. He managed to obtain a Rockefeller Foundation grant to pay her a salary at Cornell from 1933 to 1935.

term, the circumstances of her funding demonstrated the difficulties facing a woman researcher, even as talented and esteemed a scientist as McClintock. As McClintock witnessed male scientists with fewer credentials than she being appointed to good positions while she was passed by again and again, her irritation grew. Nevertheless, her commitment to science never wavered. She did advance in her work on maize genetics, and she began to be interested in the way broken maize chromosomes were able to connect themselves together again, or reanneal. Her friends in the scientific community also kept trying to find a suitable job for her—the kind of secure research position she deserved as an eminent and well-respected scientist. In 1936, Lewis Stadler succeeded, and she was appointed to an assistant professorship at the University of Missouri.

Another woman might have thought herself lucky to get the job at all and tried to accommodate herself to the prevailing expectations for a female professor by dressing conservatively, maintaining "ladylike" behavior, and expressing gratitude for her appointment. But apparently it never occurred to McClintock to behave in such a fashion. She continued dressing as she pleased and wearing her hair in a practical style then considered somewhat masculine. On one occasion, having forgotten her keys to her lab, she calmly climbed in through the window—a stunt that the college officials found unamusing. In addition, she was not a particularly successful teacher of un-

dergraduate students, for her ideas were complicated, and she grew impatient with people who could not follow them quickly.

To make her situation even more unsatisfactory, it was clear to McClintock from the start that she would never be considered equal to the male professors at the University of Missouri and had no real future there. Evelyn Fox Keller quotes McClintock as saying about her position, "I had no chance of being promoted, I was excluded from the faculty meetings. . . . I had no real part." She became increasingly aware that Missouri would not be home to her and her corn plants for long.

By 1939, McClintock had published several more papers on the ability of broken chromosomes to reanneal, and that year she was elected vice-president of the Genetics Society of America. On the strictly scientific level, her career progressed as successfully as it ever had. Her ability to correlate the physical appearance of the multicolored kernels on an ear of maize with the microscopic changes in corn cell chromosomes was unrivaled. The papers she had published since 1938 on the characteristics of reannealing maize chromosomes generated widespread interest and praise. But by 1941 she had had all she could take of the situation at the University of Missouri, and without even knowing where she would go next, she decided to take an unpaid leave of absence from the university.

At just about the same time, coincidentally, her old colleague Marcus Rhoades took a position at Columbia

University in New York City; in a letter to him, McClintock asked where he meant to grow his corn, for Manhattan was obviously not a very good place for farming. When she learned that he intended to grow maize at Cold Spring Harbor, a research center on Long Island, McClintock thought it might be a good place for her to grow her new corn crop, too. After Milislav Demerec, another geneticist who worked there, arranged for her to be invited to the center, she spent the summer of 1941 at Cold Spring Harbor.

The laboratory at Cold Spring Harbor was founded by the Carnegie Institution of Washington, itself funded by a $10 million donation from businessman and philanthropist Andrew Carnegie in 1902. The Carnegie Institution's mission, according to its charter, is to "encourage, in the broadest and most liberal manner, investigation, research, and discovery, and the application of knowledge to the improvement of mankind." Seven research centers were set up by the foundation: the Mount Wilson and Las Campanas astronomical observatories in Pasadena, California; the Geophysical Laboratory (for study of the earth's crust) and the Department of Terrestrial Magnetism (devoted to research on the earth's electrical and magnetic fields, radio waves, and physics) in Washington, D.C.; the Department of Plant Biology at Stanford; the Department of Embryology in Baltimore, Maryland; and the Department of Genetics at Cold Spring Harbor. The Department of Genetics, founded in 1904 as the first genetics laboratory in the United States, was originally called the Station for Experimental Evolution from 1904 to 1921. The Carnegie Institution supported research year-round at the Department of Genetics (as it was known from 1921 to 1962; from 1962 to 1971 it was called the Genetics Research Unit), but Cold Spring Harbor is also the site of the locally supported Long Island Biological Association, which operates during the summer. This segment of the complex traced its beginnings back to 1890, when the Brooklyn Institute of Arts and Sciences established a marine biology field station there and taught summer biology courses. By 1990, the entire complex was called the Cold Spring Harbor Laboratory.

Located about 40 miles east of New York City on the north shore of Long Island, the scientific center combined the relaxed atmosphere and beauty of an Atlantic shore summer resort with the excitement of science practiced at its highest level. Later the unit became known for cancer research, but at the time McClintock went there it was one of the most important centers for the study of genetics in the world. In his book *The Eighth Day of Creation*, science writer Horace Freeland Judson described the laboratory compound:

"Buildings are scattered either side of the road, the houses somewhat shabby, Victorian . . . the lawn slopes . . . down to a volleyball court [and] a boxy, airy, pleasant little library. Across the pretty cove . . . lies a boat basin. Meetings, meals, parties, discussions spill across the lawn or up onto the road; groups of

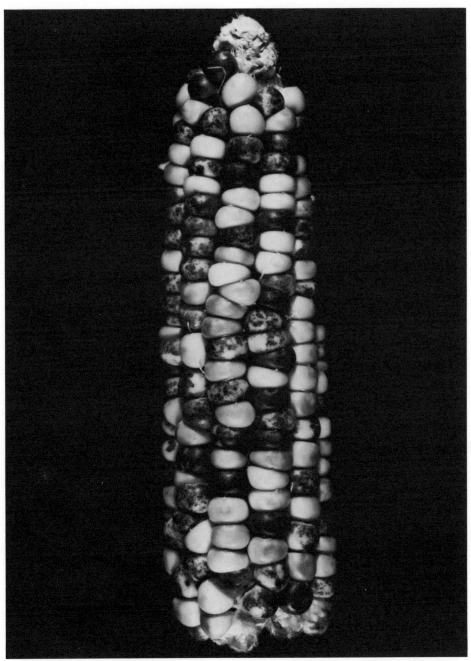

An ear of multicolored maize revealed much to McClintock. She was unrivaled in her ability to correlate the appearance of colored sectors of maize kernels with a plant's chromosomal makeup.

swimmers wander ... through the woods to the sand."

During the 1940s, eminent summer visitors to Cold Spring Harbor's scientific meetings included Salvador Luria, Max Delbruck, Jacques-Lucien Monod, Francis Crick, James Watson, and others—many of the most important geneticists of the time. During the winter, most of these scientists returned to their home labs and their university teaching jobs. McClintock, however, had no such position to which she could return.

"I came in June," she told Evelyn Fox Keller about that first year, "and when the summer was over I stayed—I liked it very much."

Even then she did not know whether or not she would be able to stay or what she would do if she had to leave. But a few months later Demerec, who was a friend of McClintock's, became director of the Carnegie Institution's genetics department, and he offered her an established research position at Cold Spring Harbor. Although the first appointment was for only one year, Demerec was able to offer her a permanent position the following year. She accepted, and Cold Spring Harbor became her home.

L. C. Dunn (left), a scientist and writer, chats with McClintock in Cold Spring Harbor in 1942. McClintock found the laboratories and atmosphere there very congenial to her work, and the research center became her home in 1941.

In 1947, McClintock prepares a slide for viewing in her microscope. The six years between 1945 and 1951 were particularly intense and productive for McClintock, as she grappled with the problems that eventually led her to discover transposable genetic regulatory elements.

FIVE

Cold Spring Harbor

The 1940s was a productive and gratifying decade for Barbara McClintock. With her 1942 appointment to the staff of Cold Spring Harbor's small year-round population of scientists, she had at last achieved a secure position in scientific research: one that was suited to her increasing importance in the scientific community and that would allow her to pursue her work without having to worry about finding a new job every few years.

During the summer, scientists of the highest ability and reputation flocked to the seaside labs to exchange ideas, present theories, and draw from each other the encouragement, enthusiasm, and understanding they could only get from fellow researchers. Science was the topic of conversation at picnics, swimming parties, and shared meals as well as in the labs, the library, and the conference halls.

Among the conferees were James Watson and Francis Crick, who would later discover the double-helix shape of the DNA molecule—the molecule that makes up genes and is thus the basis of all life. For this discovery they would share the Nobel Prize in medicine in 1962. There, too, was Max Delbruck, one of the earliest workers in the field of molecular biology (molecules are the smallest possible bits of matter; molecular biology deals with the way they behave in living beings), and his co-workers Salvador Luria and Alfred Hershey. These three would share the Nobel Prize in medicine in 1969 for their work on the viruses that infect bacteria (called phages). During the months of July, August, and September, Cold Spring Harbor swarmed with scientists.

But during the winter, Cold Spring Harbor was more like a monastery than a summer camp, with plenty of peace and quiet for serious thinking and long stretches of uninterrupted work; in fact, there were few other amusements. In the early 1940s even the meals were plain, and getting away for a break by car was not often possible because during World War II both food and gasoline were rationed by the government so that such valuable resources—and the means of producing them—could be directed toward the war effort.

Fortunately, McClintock did not mind being alone, nor did she have much taste for luxuries. After she moved to Cold Spring Harbor, her work progressed well under its isolated and somewhat spartan conditions. She published the results of her corn experiments in the Carnegie Institution's annual reports and in the scientific journal *Genetics*. Her reputation also continued to grow; in 1944, she was named president of the Genetics Society of America—the first female president in the society's history—and was named a member of the National Academy of Sciences—only the third woman in history to be elected to the academy, the nation's most prestigious scientific organization.

In that year too she received an invitation to visit her old friend George Beadle at Stanford University. He said he had a problem for her to work on: the identification and labeling of the chromosomes in *Neurospora*. (*Neurospora* is a type of red mold that grows on bread.) Others had tried and failed, for the chromosomes were too small for most people to work with at all, but

Beadle felt confident that McClintock would succeed. Such a project called on all McClintock's expertise as a cytologist. Although geneticists had tracked mutations through generations of *Neurospora*, investigators had failed in their attempts to understand its cytology—to look at the mold cells and know what was going on inside them and how the chromosomes behaved during meiosis. In fact, they could not even identify the chromosomes. Because McClintock had had such success in investigating maize cytology and correlating the appearance of maize chromosomes with the plant's genetics, Beadle thought that McClintock was the researcher who could clear up the mysteries of *Neurospora*.

She was not so sure. "I was really quite petrified," Evelyn Fox Keller quotes her as saying, "that maybe I was taking on more than I could really do." Once she began the work she became even more worried, for at first she made no progress. McClintock told her biographer that she grew frustrated and at last went out for a walk down a long road lined with eucalyptus trees. Sitting beneath them, she thought about the problem for half an hour, trying to figure out why she could not get anywhere with it.

Then, Keller quotes her: "Suddenly I jumped up. . . . I knew I was going to solve it—everything was going to be all right." She did not know why she felt this way, but upon returning to the lab she looked through the microscope again and found her moment of inspiration had changed everything. Whereas before she had seen only confusion, she recalled that "the more I worked with [the chromosomes] the bigger and bigger [they] got. . . . I was even able to see the internal parts of the chromosomes . . . as if I were right down there and these were my friends."

A few days later, she had identified the chromosomes and observed and described the meiotic process in the mold cells. So accurate were her insights and discoveries that Marcus Rhoades noted in 1969, "In the few weeks she devoted to Neurospora there resulted what remains more than twenty years later as the definitive paper on the meiotic chromosomes of this fungus." Although she knew that her work and experience as a scientist over many years had helped her in the task, she felt that her sudden inspiration under the eucalyptus trees was a key event. She had become so deeply involved with the chromosomes that she was able to forget everything else, even herself, and feel that she was almost a part of them; in this way she was able to let the chromosomes themselves guide her to truths about them. Her intuitions about the chromosomes of the maize plant now became reliable signposts, ones she could count on to direct her to new, valuable experiments of her own.

Returning to Cold Spring Harbor in 1945, she resumed her corn experiments energetically. At this point she was absorbed with the study of mutations (changes in plants caused by damage to their chromosomes)—and very peculiar mutations in particular. In one generation of maize, she observed numerous mutations in the colors of the plants' leaves: patches of different colors in a single leaf and stalk. For example, a patch of dark green might appear next to a spot of light green or yellow. A few large patches or numerous small ones might appear. Careful observation of each maize plant revealed that the rate of change remained the same throughout its growing cycle. The number and variety of changes occurred with regularity rather than at random, and McClintock theorized that something must be controlling the mutations. Fascinated by the strange ways these variegated patterns were inherited, she began trying to identify what the mutation-controlling factor might be.

For the next six years, as usual, she grew corn plants in the summer and studied them in the winter. Almost every generation of maize revealed new facets of the mutation phenomenon. She labored to understand what kind of a pattern underlay the changes and what kind of events were taking place in the plants' chromosomes. Two years after she began her investigation, she felt confident that the mutations arose from broken chromosomes and that something controlled the breakage. She surmised that there are two types of genes: structural genes that control the plant's appearance and genes that control whether these structural genes will operate. In addition, these controlling elements seemed to be able to change position. Still, the questions piled up. How did these controlling elements move, and most important, why did they move where and when they did? As she learned more and more, her theory of the way the cells' mutations were controlled grew increasingly complex—so complex, in fact, that no one else was able to understand it. Her understanding of the corn cells' inner workings had advanced far beyond even that of other maize geneticists—in part because she was allowing her own well-trained intuitions to guide her toward what experiments she ought to do next. What to others might appear to be "jumping to conclusions" was in fact a carefully thought out series of steps, based on a detailed mass of knowledge that no one else had.

At the time, other scientists believed that genes were fixed in their places on chromosomes—that they did not move. But by the late 1940s, McClintock disagreed with this idea completely. Basically, her theory held that a piece of chromosome—a controlling element—could break away from the chromosome, or dissociate, and be reinserted in another place near a structural gene. By turning structural genes on or off they caused the type of mutations she observed, among others. What controlled the movement of controlling elements were parts of the chromosome itself: She called the locus (place) on a chromosome that triggered breakage the *Ds* locus and the element that triggered Ds activity the *Ac* factor. McClintock delved even deeper into the phenomenon to discover how Ac regulates itself. Her complete theory is dense and closely reasoned, and a thorough knowledge of genetics is neces-

sary in order to understand it and the steps that lead to her final, fully worked out theory. At last she concluded that genetic elements can change position within and between chromosomes and that such changes are regulated and systematic. She called the process transposition.

In the late 1940s, however, other scientists did not call it anything, because they did not understand it. McClintock had been publishing brief reports of her work on the movable controlling elements of chromosomes only in the Carnegie Institution's annual reports; she wanted to complete her theory before presenting it to the scientific community. She knew there would be some resistance to it. "I went overboard," Evelyn Fox Keller quotes her as saying, "collecting evidence . . . until there was absolutely no doubt."

In 1951, at the annual summer Cold Spring Harbor Symposium, the moment came at last for her to present her theory of genetic transposition along with the evidence for it to her colleagues. Wearing a plain shirt and crisply pressed slacks, she stepped to the front of the lecture hall. Brushing back her short, dark hair, the 49-year-old scientist glanced at her notes, then up at her assembled audience, and at last began a speech that, if successful, would change the world's view of the science of genetics. But if it failed—as it might, for there was no guarantee other scientists would understand or accept her work—her career in science could be ruined.

As she outlined her views to the

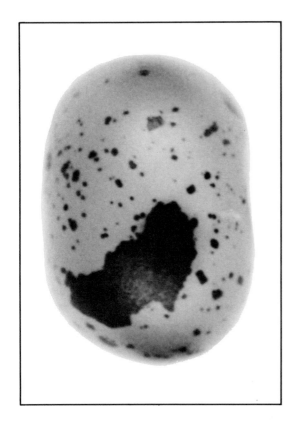

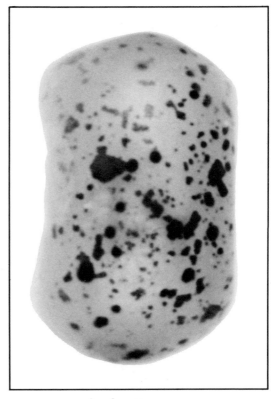

Two maize kernels show very different patterns of coloration. Investigating the pattern behind the differences in pigmentation in maize stalks and leaves proved to be exceedingly demanding and complex, but McClintock persevered in her effort to understand what caused and regulated such variations.

audience, it seemed at first that she was communicating well with them. As her voice gained strength and her face took on animation, they listened to every word. She was, she told them, absolutely certain the changes she had detected in the chromosomes were real. She described the system by which they must occur and offered the huge mass of evidence she had gathered to support her conclusions.

Meanwhile, however, the interest on

the faces of her listeners changed first to confusion and then to contempt. Now she realized that her worst fears about this presentation were coming true: Despite all her evidence, her theory was just too radical, too complicated, too new, and too unusual for her audience to accept. Nevertheless, McClintock kept speaking, trying to communicate her facts.

When she finished, there were no comments and no applause, only silence. Stunned by the obvious dismissal of her work, McClintock left the podium to the sounds of whispers, muttered scorn, even laughter. She had failed utterly. In the days that followed, only three scientists asked for a printed copy of her speech, and word spread in the scientific world: McClintock's

McClintock (seated, third from left) was among old friends Rollins Emerson (standing, fourth from left), Milislav Demerec (standing, sixth from left), Lewis Stadler (seated, third from right), Curt Stern (seated, second from right), and Marcus Rhoades (seated, far right) at the Gene Conference of 1949, held in May and June on Shelter Island, New York. Her work on transposition and regulation was progressing during this period, but she did not present it in full to the scientific community until the Cold Spring Harbor Symposium of 1951.

work was not only impossible to understand; it was also just plain wrong. McClintock, people said, had become some kind of scientific oddball whose work simply could not be taken seriously. Some suggested she might even be losing her mind.

There are several reasons why she experienced such complete rejection. First, because she had not published much about her theory, it was extremely new to her audience. Second, because her ideas were so complex and her presentation dense and closely reasoned, the audience found her speech difficult to follow. Third, her way of working was different from theirs; unlike scientists at large university research centers, McClintock worked alone and allowed her incredibly intense concentration to guide her in ways they had not experienced. Thus they found the research that led to her results difficult to comprehend. Fourth, her theory went entirely against the then-believed ideas about how chromosomes behaved. Fifth, the organism she worked with, maize, was not as popular a subject for research as it had been; so many researchers were ill equipped to understand the intricacies of its genetics. And, finally, she was a woman—certainly not the most important reason for her rejection, but a contributing factor to it. McClintock could not even demonstrate the truth of her theory by asking other scientists to look through the microscope to see what she had seen. No one else had her highly developed powers of observation or her 30 years of intense familiarity with the corn cells' inner workings. That was the point of her presentation: to explain what she had seen, and what she had reasoned from her observations. Not that anyone wanted her to attempt such a demonstration: "I don't want to hear a thing about what you're doing," Evelyn Fox Keller quotes one scientist who visited Cold Spring Harbor after 1951 as saying to McClintock. "It may be interesting, but I understand it's kind of mad."

After her disastrous 1951 effort at Cold Spring Harbor, she tried to present her theory to smaller audiences at a number of seminars. Marshaling even more statistics from the immense amounts of data she had accumulated, she added these results to an explanation of her theory in an article she wrote for *Genetics*, which was published in 1953. A stunning lack of response greeted her attempt to reach an interested audience. Recognition of her theory's validity and importance failed to come from the community of scientists. Frustrated by her inability to communicate ideas that were, to her, so obvious, she withdrew into her laboratory, continuing her research as intensely as ever but not publishing papers about it except in the Carnegie annual reports. She had tried and failed to get her ideas across; now she put all her energies into the work itself and let attempts to communicate it to others fall by the wayside.

She knew she was right: Mutations were regulated by a system of controls that were part of the corn chromosomes. Genetic elements did indeed

rearrange themselves on chromosomes. Sooner or later, she hoped, other scientists would come to understand these things, too. Meanwhile, she kept working, alone and silently but with continuing pleasure in the research itself.

Even as McClintock's ideas were being rejected, though, the new science of molecular biology was becoming more and more central to other scientists' study of genetics. Rather than observing the relationship between changes in a plant's appearance and the changes deep within its cells, molecular biologists studied how molecules—bits of matter that formed chemicals, which in turn formed genes and chromosomes—acted. It was from these techniques that the majority of geneticists expected new knowledge to come. McClintock and her discoveries seemed to have been bypassed in the rush down a different avenue of scientific research.

An aerial view of Cold Spring Harbor shows the seaside laboratories. After other scientists failed to understand McClintock's presentation on transposition in 1951, she made only a few more efforts to convince them at small seminars and spent most of her time at the Cold Spring Harbor laboratories, delving deeper into the fascinating problem of genetic regulation.

McClintock in 1960. Throughout the 1960s, evidence supporting McClintock's theories mounted, and she received a number of scientific awards and honors. However, other scientists still did not fully grasp the significance of her work.

S I X

A Modern Mendel

When Gregor Mendel first proposed his accurate observations about heredity in pea plants in 1866, scientists showed no interest. The scientific community at the time was in an upheaval over Charles Darwin and his 1859 book, *On the Origin of Species by Means of Natural Selection*, in which he presented his theory of evolution and explanation of its operation. He postulated three mechanisms by which the process of evolution operated: heredity, wherein members of a species pass on their features to succeeding generations; variety, or mutation, through which new features of a species arise; and natural selection, whereby new characteristics become dominant through the influence of the environment on survival of individuals. Although Mendel's findings clearly explained the operation of heredity, one of the most crucial processes in evolu-

tion, a crushing lack of interest greeted his work. His rules, now known as the laws of Mendelian inheritance, are completely accepted by scientists today, but in 1866 they were so new and so unfamiliar that they seemed outlandish and received little serious attention from other scientists of Mendel's time. His work was ignored and then forgotten until 1900, when three European botanists each performed experiments on their own and made observations that forced them to come to the same conclusions as Mendel had. Only then did they learn he had preceded them by nearly 40 years in discovering the laws of heredity and give him credit for his work.

What happened to Barbara McClintock in the 1950s was in some ways similar. Like Mendel, who did his work in a monastery garden in a small Austrian town, she was somewhat isolated from her peers. Like him, she found herself unable to get her colleagues to understand her work or its significance. And like Mendel, she did not persist in attempting to convince them. They had to find out for themselves, years later, that they had been ignoring a theory of importance.

But unlike Mendel, who upon remaining utterly unrecognized gave up his research to become more involved in running the monastery where he lived, McClintock did not stop her experiments or lose her enthusiasm for them. To McClintock the goal of achieving her colleagues' acceptance was one thing, and the work itself was quite another. It was the work itself and nothing else that fascinated her. "It was *fun*," Horace Freeland Judson quotes her as saying to him. Even after her theories had been rejected by other scientists, "I couldn't wait to get up in the morning," she said.

Her research continued to be fruitful. At the Brookhaven Symposium in 1955 she presented supporting evidence for another system of gene regulation and control that she uncovered. Despite reams of evidence and her own best efforts, her 1951 Cold Spring Harbor presentation on the Ds-Ac system and transposition had failed to convince the majority of geneticists that either phenomenon existed, in part because the ideas themselves were exceedingly complex and her speech was even more so. Undaunted, she spoke about the second system she uncovered, which she named the *Spm* system. McClintock asserted that the system con-

sisted of a suppressor component that regulated a mutator component, and like Ds and Ac, these components could also move from place to place on genes—that is, undergo transposition. To an audience that could not accept her assertion that the Ds-Ac system existed and functioned as she said, her explanation of the Spm system was as incomprehensible as her earlier presentation and of as little interest.

The following year, in 1956, McClintock stood before another group of scientists assembled for the Cold Spring Harbor Symposium. She not only elaborated her understanding of the Ds-Ac system but also presented her discovery and elucidation of the Spm system. Her speech was even more complicated and dense than the one she had given five years earlier. The audience was more dismissive and even less interested than five years earlier. Even for the very few—a small number of maize geneticists and a couple of interested colleagues at Cold Spring Harbor, such as Evelyn Witkin—who had understood and remained interested in her work, the complexity of the ideas and the logical progression of hypotheses in her 1956 presentation demanded close attention and much thought in order for them to follow her discoveries. For those who had not comprehended her earlier work, the presentation was nearly impossible to fathom and was further proof of her wrongheadedness. Their reception was cool, if not hostile. Disappointed in her co-workers' inability to acknowledge the importance of her work, she did not

McClintock and one of her oldest friends, Harriet Creighton, at the Cold Spring Harbor Symposium of 1956, where McClintock presented data supporting the existence of a second system of genetic regulation. To her frustration, the overwhelming majority of the audience again did not comprehend her presentation.

speak again about her research until 1960, although she continued to reap rewards of her own at the microscope and in the cornfield.

Scientists showed little or no interest in McClintock's studies of cytology and heredity, but two years earlier, in 1954, they had been electrified by other discoveries affecting the field of genetics. Fewer and fewer geneticists studied the chromosomes of cells under the microscope and the patterns of heredity in maize or in *Drosophila*. Instead, they studied bacteria, for new instruments enabled them to study the tiny, one-celled organisms that reproduced not in a matter of months or even in days but rather in a matter of hours. Many researchers did most of their work on the molecular biology of bacteria, and Cold Spring Harbor was the site of numerous studies of this type. Some

James D. Watson and Francis Crick explaining a model of the double-helix structure of DNA. Watson and Crick shared the 1962 Nobel Prize in medicine or physiology with Maurice Wilkins for their discovery of DNA's structure.

scientists centered their investigations in particular on the biochemical units of heredity. In the 1940s, researchers had discovered that DNA (deoxyribonucleic acid) was the molecule that carried genetic material, and in the April 25, 1953, issue of the scientific journal *Nature*, Francis Crick and James Watson announced that they had uncovered the double-helix structure of DNA that enables it to replicate and pass on genetic information. Soon, investigators demonstrated that particular sequences of chemicals in DNA encoded the information that enabled cells to create specific proteins and thus pass on genetic traits. The focus of genetics had shifted away from the subjects that fascinated McClintock.

Nevertheless, she kept herself well informed on the progress of other scientists. And in 1960 she read a paper by a pair of French scientists, Jacques-Lucien Monod and François Jacob of the Pasteur Institute in Paris, published in a French journal, *Comptes Rendus*, that excited her tremendously. In it Jacob and Monod described a system of regulation they had observed in the genes of a common bacteria called *Escherichia coli* that is found in human intestines, among other places—a system very much like the one McClintock had first described in maize genes back in 1951.

The methods the French scientists had used for studying their bacteria were utterly unlike McClintock's methods of studying corn chromosomes. Simply put, she observed the whole plants, then observed their chromosomes and genes through a microscope, and then figured out the relationship between what the plant did and what its genes were doing. Molecular biologists such as Jacob and Monod, on the other hand, used extremely sophisticated new scientific instruments such as the electron microscope to study the tiniest and most basic bits of matter that make up living things: molecules, atoms, and subatomic particles such as protons and electrons. (Instead of using visible light and glass lenses to magnify objects, the electron microscope uses a beam of electrons to illuminate the objects and magnifies their image with magnetic fields.) It was with the use of such techniques that Jacob and Monod discovered gene-regulating systems in bacteria. In keeping with the overwhelming interest in molecular biology among geneticists, they centered their research on finding a molecular basis for gene regulation and concentrated on the system that turns the genes on and off when they create proteins.

Despite the differences in techniques and focus, however, the similarities between the results of Jacob and Monod and those of McClintock herself were too great for her to ignore. At once, she told her colleagues at Cold Spring Harbor about this event. She composed a paper about it, "Some Parallels Between Gene Control Systems in Maize and in Bacteria," for a scientific journal, *The American Naturalist*, and wrote to Monod informing him of the similarities between his and Jacob's work and her own.

They had not known of these similarities. "They did not understand the technical aspects of maize genetics," McClintock told Horace Freeland Judson in explanation. And they had not found the moving genes McClintock had discussed in her own work, only nonmoving regulators of genetic activity. But the regulating systems alone represented enormously significant points of comparison between their work and hers, and upon reading her new paper Monod and Jacob realized this at once. That summer, at the 1961 Cold Spring Harbor Symposium, they credited McClintock with having discovered more than 10 years earlier systems of gene regulation in maize similar to the ones they had just now found in bacteria.

For Monod and Jacob, their work on *E. coli* bacteria would lead to the Nobel Prize in physiology or medicine in 1965. For McClintock, it meant her ideas were finally beginning to be seen as right: What the "new science" of molecular biology was revealing was precisely what she had been saying all along. Unfortunately, this was not widely realized at first; it was the findings of Jacob and Monod that got most of the attention at the 1961 symposium, not their similarity to McClintock's work. To other scientists it was the discoveries coming out of molecular biology that were important, not proving that McClintock had been correct.

Meanwhile, McClintock's own life and work continued with little change. She lived simply at Cold Spring Harbor,

devoting the majority of her time and energy to research on the regulation of genes in maize. She made an exception in her highly specialized studies of her own corn only during the winters from 1958 to 1960. The break must have been welcome because times were hard for McClintock then. During those years she was delving into the exceedingly complex Spm system, and she had not yet recognized any parallels between her work and that of any other researchers. The period was productive but lonely. During those two winters, she traveled to South America to assist in a National Academy of Sciences project on identifying and preserving the native strains of corn there.

On the trips, McClintock rapidly grasped the essentials of Spanish conversation and met many new scientists. More important, although the work was far removed from studying genetic regulation and control, her ability to look at data and discern an underlying pattern aided her in the project. Corn most probably originated in the Americas, and native species had been a staple of the diet of Native Americans for thousands of years. They had bred the corn that fit their needs most closely by selecting seeds from the plants they preferred and planting them the following season. European explorers and settlers had bred and crossbred many different varieties, and advances in corn breeding by the 20th century had produced numerous varieties of cultivated corn with characteristics far removed from those of native varieties. In fact, the spread of cultivated corn

Jacques-Lucien Monod (left) and François Jacob (right) published a paper in 1960 that excited McClintock tremendously. (Andre Lwoff, standing between Monod and Jacob, shared the 1965 Nobel Prize in medicine or physiology with them.) In their 1960 paper, they discussed their discovery of genetic regulatory elements in bacteria. McClintock immediately grasped the parallels between their work and hers, but other scientists were slower to see the similarities.

threatened to make the native varieties extinct, and the National Academy of Sciences project was devoted to finding and preserving native varieties for future study. In examining the chromosomal differences between native varieties and various more highly bred varieties in different geographic locations, McClintock discovered it was possible to trace how different civilizations had moved, expanded, and died out, for each group or civilization had tended to grow particular, chromosomally distinct types in its own area, and the corn that Native Americans had grown and bred cannot grow without human cultivation. As each group migrated, so did its maize. But once she had trained South American scientists to do the work that was necessary, McClintock returned to New York and her own research—for which she still had received little recognition.

At Brookhaven again in 1965, McClintock presented results of her research on transposition at the symposium to the same frustrating lack of response. Gradually, however, by 1965 a sort of undercurrent of support for McClintock began, as other scientists were slowly confirming more and more aspects of her work. In bacteria, for example, molecular biologists found first that viruses could carry parts of

McClintock poses with co-workers at an agricultural school in Peru. In the late 1950s, she traveled in South America on a project sponsored by the National Academy of Sciences.

genes from one place on a chromosome to many other places on it. This was important because (except for McClintock) they had previously thought parts of genes could only be moved to a few specific places. Next, they found movable genetic elements like the ones she had found in corn—not parts of genes being carried by viruses but moving on their own, as McClintock had said they did.

The result was not any sort of public "she was right all along" statement; for one thing, the other scientists were still not particularly interested in whether or not McClintock had been correct, but in their own research and careers. For another, they did not yet

McClintock looks over data with two colleagues in Mexico City in November 1966. From 1963 to 1969 she was a consultant in agricultural science to the Rockefeller Foundation. McClintock remained involved with the worldwide scientific community and received a number of awards during the late 1960s.

have enough evidence to make such an admission. That movable genetic elements had been found in one kind of bacteria, for example, did not convince molecular biologists that these elements were also present in maize, and they had not yet discovered any evidence of their own to support this idea (although later they would find such evidence).

By the middle of the 1960s, however, McClintock did begin to receive considerable public honors and recognition: In 1965, Cornell University awarded her an honorary professorship; in 1967, she received the National Academy of Sciences' Kimber Genetics Award, and in 1970 she received the National Medal of Science. Meanwhile, evidence for her position was uncov-

ered little by little by scientists working with the methods of molecular biology. The process was slow, however, and McClintock did not find the awards she received in the 1960s adequate compensation for the disappointment she felt about the failure of other scientists to comprehend her discoveries. She did not strive to be recognized personally for her achievements; she wanted her discoveries to be recognized and understood. By 1970, when she won the National Medal of Science, nearly 20 years had passed since her first attempt to communicate to her colleagues that the phenomena of genetic regulation and transposition in maize chromosomes existed. At long last, that frustrating state of affairs was about to change.

McClintock works at her desk at Cold Spring Harbor Laboratory in 1971. She meticulously documented all her findings and continued writing papers for the Carnegie Institute's annual reports as evidence supporting her discovery of movable regulatory genetic elements grew.

SEVEN

Waiting for the World to Catch Up

McClintock knew that she had observed transposition in maize chromosomes, but she had been unable to convince other researchers, for many lacked her understanding of maize genetics. More familiar with the study of genetics in bacteria and molecular biology, they could only be convinced by finding confirmation of the process in the organisms that they peered at through the microscope. Slowly during the 1960s and more quickly during the 1970s, evidence supporting the existence of transposition accumulated.

Several researchers, including Francis Crick, found that one of the most interesting ways to study the DNA in bacteria was to look at the behavior of bacteriophages and bacteria. A bacteriophage is a virus, which is so simple in structure that it spans the difference between a living and nonliving thing. Viruses are not cells, as bacteria are;

rather, they consist of a few genes carried inside an outer coating of protein. Bacteriophages are parasites that attach themselves to bacteria and take over the much more complex systems of the bacterial cell, including the system by which cells produce proteins. They reproduce by directing the bacteria to produce copies of their own DNA and the type of protein coat they consist of, and then they burst open the bacterial cell. The many newly released copies of the original virus then attach themselves to other cells and repeat the process. Crick concentrated on using bacteriophages to begin to determine the particular chemical sequences in DNA that determine what kind of amino acids (the building blocks of which proteins are made) will be produced. Other researchers observed different aspects of the interaction between bacteriophages and bacteria, including the phenomenon of transduction.

Scientists did not challenge the existence of transduction, which had been proven to occur in bacteria. Molecular biologists had found that viruses could insert themselves into bacteria and sometimes carried parts of genes from one place on a chromosome to another. In 1963, A. J. Taylor published a paper in the *Proceedings of the National Academy of Sciences* in which he described one particular type of bacteriophage that caused mutations in *E. coli*. The bacteriophage could insert itself into many places on a bacterial chromosome—perhaps at any place. This discovery changed the mind of researchers who had previously thought only a few specific places on the chromosome would accept the insertion of bacteriophage DNA. In 1966 three researchers observed the same sort of phenomenon with another bit of matter that is much like a virus. These three researchers, Jonathan Beckwith, Ethan Signer, and Wolfgang Epstein actually used the word *transposition* in their published work, although they did not refer to McClintock or her research.

By the latter part of the 1960s, scientists working with mutations in *E. coli* observed changes that occurred not as a result of X rays or other agents that usually cause mutations; instead, they seemed to occur because of an abnormal arrangement of genes on a chromosome. The mutations were finally ascertained to be a consequence of the insertion of one of several very specific

segments of DNA called insertion sequences. However, the DNA in insertion sequences neither came from nor was carried by a foreign organism such as a bacteriophage but instead originated from a different place on the chromosome and moved on its own. These sequences also occasionally carried bits of DNA from nearby parts of the gene, which caused exactly the kinds of rearrangements of chromosomes that McClintock had observed in maize. The way in which these researchers approached this field of inquiry differed from McClintock's work in one very important aspect and partially explains why many still did not see the relevance of McClintock's findings to their own. Biologists investigating insertion sequences concentrated on the molecular structure that identified the sequences and allowed them to operate—to cut themselves out of one chromosome and insert themselves in another place on the chromosome or an entirely different chromosome. McClintock had observed how transposable elements function and the kind of mutations they gave rise to, not how their molecules were structured.

Excited by the work being done on the movement of genetic material, more and more scientists devoted their time to carrying out experiments to advance their knowledge of this curious process. Some of their work had immediate practical implications. Late in the 1960s, a number of researchers were investigating how *Salmonella* bacteria, which cause severe food poisoning in humans, could quickly become resistant to the antibiotic drugs used to kill them. The time it took for *Salmonella* to become resistant to the antibiotics doctors prescribed for treatment was surprisingly short. How could the genetic information be passed on so rapidly? The answer lay in the ability of the antibiotic-resistant gene to move easily from place to place on the chromosome, between chromosomes and plasmids (small, separate loops of DNA in bacteria), and (by way of bacteriophages) from bacterium to bacterium. This ease of movement allowed the genetic information to spread at a great rate of speed. Researchers found that these kinds of movable genetic elements performed much as the ones McClintock had found in corn. These genes and genetic elements were not always or exclusively carried by viruses; they moved on their own as McClintock had said they did in maize.

In 1972, Peter Starlinger and Heinz Saedler compared the behavior of insertion sequences to the movable genetic elements McClintock had described. Finally, four years later at a meeting at Cold Spring Harbor devoted in part to insertion sequences, it was proposed that all segments of DNA that can insert themselves in various places on chromosomes be called transposable elements. At last, the term McClintock had introduced at Cold Spring Harbor a quarter century earlier was being used to mean just what she meant it to: parts of genes that can move from one spot on a chromosome to another.

Yet the differences between maize

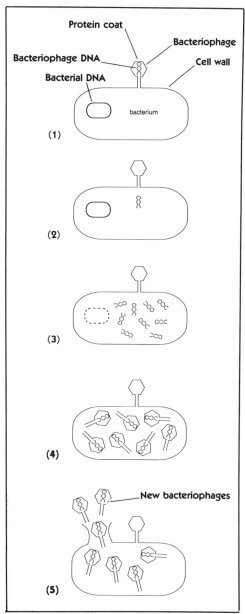

A schematic diagram depicts a bacteriophage reproducing itself by using the biochemical machinery of a bacterium. Genetic researchers in the 1960s and 1970s concentrated on the study of these simple organisms.

and bacteria that had prevented many researchers from understanding McClintock's work or seeing its parallels to their own still blocked the way to a full acceptance of her theories. Bacteria are simple one-celled organisms; maize plants are complex individuals made up of many specialized cells. Bacteria are prokaryotic, that is, they have no nucleus that holds chromosomal material; maize, like other multicellular life forms, is eukaryotic, that is, it has a clearly defined nucleus and a much more complex system of cellular organization. These features are among those that make bacteria good for genetic research and easy for molecular biologists to study but also make them very unlike higher plants and animals. The differences between bacteria and higher organisms are so great that scientists hesitated before claiming that the chromosomal processes they observed in bacteria took place in more complicated living things.

In the 1970s, while work on drug-resistant *Salmonella* was going on, Saedler (who had observed an analogy between McClintock's discoveries and insertion sequences five years earlier)

Although McClintock continued her own highly specialized investigations at her microscope and in her cornfields, she never failed to keep up with the latest work in genetics. As the 1960s progressed, she found that support for her ideas occasionally came from unexpected sources, such as research on drug-resistant Salmonella *bacteria.*

and another researcher, Patricia Nevers, applied themselves to the task of understanding McClintock's system of research and the complexities of maize genetics. In 1977, the two scientists published a paper in the highly respected scientific journal *Nature* that pointed out the parallels and likenesses between transposition in maize and in bacteria and made maize genetics clearer to researchers familiar with bacteria.

By the beginning of the 1980s, researchers had identified transposable genetic elements not only in bacteria but also in yeasts and *Drosophila*; their existence had gone from farfetched idea to accepted fact. Journalists referred to them as "jumping genes" in newspaper and magazine articles. Finally, McClintock's work was recognized by the scientific community. In 1981 (quoted by Evelyn Fox Keller from an article by Jean Marx in *Science* magazine) scientist Melvin Green of the University of California at Davis said, "They [movable genetic elements] are everywhere . . . perhaps even in mice and men."

McClintock continued to pursue her research while other scientists discovered and proved to themselves that she had been right so many years ago. She presented a paper entitled "Mechanisms That Rapidly Reorganize the Genome" in 1978 at a symposium in which she tackled the larger issues raised by her research on transposition, regulation, and control. In 1980 she wrote another paper, "Modified Gene Expressions Induced by Transposable Elements," in which she made some startling propositions about the implications of transposable elements and their effect on evolution. She did work on the influence of transposable and controlling elements on an organism's development, which, like her work in the 1950s, was exceedingly complex. Few could understand, but she had survived the incomprehension of her colleagues earlier in her career, and, as ever, she remained fascinated by the work she was doing.

However, the transposable elements McClintock had described so long ago were finally fascinating others as well. If acceptance can be measured by the number of awards won, then 1981 was the year McClintock's movable genetic elements were officially endorsed by the scientific establishment, 30 years after her first presentation of the idea at Cold Spring Harbor. In that year, at the age of 79, she won 8 awards, including a $15,000 basic medical research award from the Albert Lasker Foundation, a $50,000 award from the Wolf Foundation in Israel, and a $60,000 per year tax-free lifetime stipend from the John B. and Catherine D. MacArthur Foundation.

In announcing the award to McClintock, the MacArthur Foundation reported to the *New York Times* that her discovery of movable genetic elements was the "basis for today's research in gene exploration," and that she was a pioneer of "new . . . subtle . . . and complex genetic theories that are as yet only dimly understood."

Those honors were more than McClintock had ever received, and the

A building on the Cold Spring Harbor Laboratory grounds that originally housed animals was officially named the Barbara McClintock Laboratory in 1973.

money was more than she had ever had. But the sudden wealth and fame did not impress her. For four decades she had lived quite contentedly in a two-room apartment over a garage at Cold Spring Harbor. She rarely bought new clothes—for her solitary work, she hardly ever needed them—and had never been interested in owning anything beyond the basic necessities. She had never wanted to be bothered by having lots of possessions; she was too busy with her work to care about owning things. And after all her years of solitude, she confessed, she found applause discomforting.

"I want to be free of all that," she told a *New York Times* reporter after the Lasker award was announced. "I'm an anonymous person." What she did want to do, she said, was more research, "because people have not yet grasped what I tried to say so many years ago . . . I mean to do it before my time is up."

She must have realized, however, that whether she liked it or not, more applause was very likely in her future.

On November 18, 1981, McClintock was formally presented with the
Lasker Award for Basic Medical Research from the Albert and Mary
Lasker Foundation, one of three major awards she received that year.
The trophy was accompanied by a prize of $15,000, and many
considered it a precursor to the Nobel Prize.

At the press conference she agreed to hold after winning the Lasker award, she looked somewhat miserable posing for a photograph. Small and slender, her short brown hair unstyled, wearing a plain white blouse, dark sweater, and a single tiny gold chain, she smiled bright-eyed but rather grimly from behind a pair of rimless spectacles.

"I don't like publicity at all," she told the gathered reporters, among whom were those writing an article for the November 30, 1981, issue of *Newsweek*. "All I want to do is retire to a quiet place in the laboratory. . . . I don't like big labs or offices."

Other scientists were not so modest on her behalf. Based on insights provided by her work, "We may see how cells change from one type to another . . . how normal development is controlled," said Dr. James Darnell of New York's Rockefeller University in a *Newsweek* article. "We could . . . learn how cancer results when a normal cell's development is upset."

For a November 30, 1981, article on McClintock in *Time* magazine, Nobel Prize winner James Watson agreed: "She is a . . . remarkable person, fiercely independent, beholden to no one. Her work is of fundamental importance."

And, as the news articles of the time were also quick to point out, the Lasker award was an almost sure sign of bigger things to come. In the past, 33 scientists who had won the Lasker prize had also gone on to win the Nobel Prize; to receive the Lasker was seen as a stepping-stone to the Nobel. Although there were several obstacles remaining in the way of her receiving the Nobel Prize—the most important and prestigious honor a scientist can achieve—in 1981 they were nowhere near as large as the ones 79-year-old Barbara McClintock had already overcome.

Steven Dellaporta (right), a molecular biologist, began working with McClintock in 1983. Molecular biologists had pursued a different path in genetic research than McClintock had, but Dellaporta planned to try to join the two strands of inquiry. He began planting seeds from McClintock's crops and investigating the molecular structure and development of the transposable genetic elements that she had discovered 30 years earlier.

EIGHT

Acclaim at Last

When Barbara McClintock won the Nobel Prize in 1983, she made Nobel history in several ways. Nobel Prizes were first awarded in 1901 in the fields of medicine or physiology (the two fields are considered one category by the Nobel awards committee), physics, chemistry, literature, and peace. An award for economics was established in 1969. By 1983, more than 350 people had received Nobel Prizes in the 3 science categories, but of all these award recipients only 6 had been women. And of these six—only two of whose prizes were in medicine or physiology—five, including Marie Curie, who also won a Nobel on her own, had shared the prize with other scientists. (When more than one scientist participates in award-winning work, the Nobel is often given to the co-workers together.)

When McClintock received the award, she became only the seventh woman in history to win a Nobel Prize in science at all, just the third to win such a prize unshared, and the very first woman ever to be awarded an unshared Nobel in the category of medicine or physiology. (The other two women to earn Nobel science awards alone received their prizes in the chemistry category: Marie Curie in 1911 for her work on radioactivity and Dorothy Hodgkin in 1964 for her work on the structure of penicillin and vitamin B_{12}.)

To become eligible for the Nobel Prize, one must first be nominated by other eminent scientists, most of them previous winners of the award themselves. The winners of the medicine or physiology award are chosen from among the nominees by members of Sweden's Karolinska Institute, whose discussions on the subject are never made public. No one outside the committee knew whether or not Mc-Clintock would receive the award until the winners were announced.

Certainly it became clear in 1981, when she received the Lasker award, that McClintock might be in line for the Nobel. But until the moment her award became public knowledge on October 10, 1983, there was much uncertainty over whether she would be honored by the Nobel committee. A number of factors seemed to be against her. For one thing, the award had been established to honor work accomplished during the previous year—not for discoveries actually made 40 years earlier, as McClintock's had been. (This rule, however, has been broken more frequently in recent times as science becomes more complex and research takes longer to complete.) In addition, her gender made her—at least to judge by the award's history—a long shot. Finally, her work on the genetics of corn did not fit well into any of the Nobel's three science categories. It was certainly not chemistry or physics, and the award for medicine or physiology was usually given to honor work on treating diseases in human beings or for research into the biology of animals, not plants.

Nevertheless, on October 10, 1983, the announcement was made. In an event unprecedented in scientific history, for her work on movable genetic elements in the maize plant, Barbara McClintock became the first woman to win a Nobel Prize in medicine or physiology entirely on her own.

"I think this is the first Nobel prize given for work originally done in higher plants," said Eugene Fox, a scientist from the ARCO Plant Cell Research Institute in California. His remarks were reported in *Science News* magazine in an article on McClintock published just three days after her award was announced. He went on to note, though, that the Nobel was not given to her until it became clear that transposable genetic elements also existed in animals, not only in plants.

In making the award, members of the Karolinska Institute committee pointed out several other important factors in their decision to give the prize to McClintock. First, they said, they had decided to award the prize to McClintock alone because she had done the work alone, at a time when other scientists did not understand her findings. The committee members mentioned the extraordinary length of time it took for her to receive the recognition she deserved, comparing her to Gregor Mendel and saying she had been "far ahead" of the discoveries made about genetics by molecular biologists. When she made her findings, commented one committee member, "only about five geneticists in the world could appreciate them, because of the complexity of the work."

Other scientists agreed. Said one senior Cold Spring Harbor researcher, Thomas Broker, she "ranks up with Darwin in understanding evolution." James Watson, by then director of Cold Spring Harbor's laboratories, remarked: "It is not a controversial award. No one thinks of genetics now without [also thinking of] the implications of her work."

Asked if she herself was bitter over the long period during which she received little attention, McClintock replied forthrightly for an article in the December 1983 issue of *Discover* magazine: "No, no, no, I don't have any bitterness at all. I mean that seriously." She had, in fact, actively discouraged the public attention that began coming her way as early as 1981; all she had ever wanted was the understanding of her colleagues, she noted, not fame or fortune.

For example, an October 16, 1983, *New York Times* article documents that when McClintock learned of author Evelyn Fox Keller's intention to write a book about her, she broke off talks with Dr. Keller and "all [Keller's] subsequent communications were carried on through a relative of Dr. McClintock." When the *Times* reporter asked McClintock about Keller's book, *A Feeling for the Organism*, McClintock said, "I want nothing to do with a book about me. I do not like publicity. . . . I have received but not read Dr. Keller's book."

Once the publicity over the Nobel Prize had faded, McClintock got her wish: to have the peace and quiet in which she could resume her work. She returned to her maize research at Cold Spring Harbor, where the only new things she acquired with all the prize money she had won were a larger apartment—she did not buy a house—and a small practical car so that she could get around more easily.

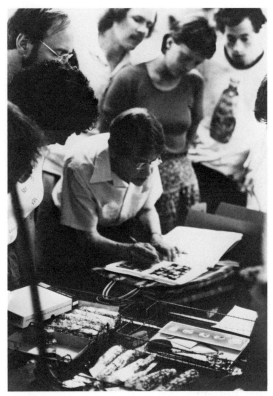

A crowd of students clusters around McClintock, then 79 years old, at a plant course she taught at Cold Spring Harbor in 1981. Although she had worked quietly and alone for years, the awards she received in 1981 made her name familiar to a new generation of scientists.

The Cold Spring Harbor Research Center is now home to investigations in a number of different scientific disciplines. In 1968, Cold Spring Harbor gained a reputation for the study of the molecular basis of cancer, which it maintained for the next two decades. In 1990, the complex was preparing for

On June 22, 1982, McClintock (second from right) attended the presentation of honorary degrees at Cambridge University in England. The ceremony, presided over by Prince Philip (center), husband of Queen Elizabeth of England, marked one of numerous honors accorded McClintock in the early 1980s.

the construction of a center devoted to neuroscience. But one of the most important ongoing projects housed at the laboratories is the National Institutes of Health's National Center for Human Genome Research, directed by James Watson. (The human genome is the set of all the genes that make up the full complement of human chromosomes.) Watson heads an ambitious and controversial project, estimated to cost $3 billion and last 15 years. The program is designed to create a complete map of the 3 billion biochemical components that make up the estimated 100,000 human genes. McClintock, however, goes on living on the grounds and working there on her corn experiments, as a distinguished service member of and

an independent investigator for the Carnegie Institution.

Working with her since 1982 has been a young molecular biologist, Dr. Steven Dellaporta, who has studied in detail McClintock's more than 50 years of research on maize. Using plants grown from seeds she has given him (she also gives seeds to other scientists who ask for them), he plans to isolate the movable parts of maize genes that she identified decades ago. Once he has done so he means to clone (reproduce) them in the lab in order to study their molecular structure.

"We have to find out more about the nature of the gene," McClintock said of such work in a February 1984 article in *Science Digest*, "what controls its ac-tion, what's behind it. I think we have a long way to go."

McClintock herself has become interested in recent years in how maize genes react to such stresses as temperature change or disruptions in the plant's nutrition. She has found that parts of genes may move more quickly when such stresses are present and wonders whether this may account for rapid changes in the evolution of some species of plant and animal life. She continues her lifelong habit of reading widely, not only in scientific journals but also on such subjects as Eastern religions, biofeedback techniques (the ability to learn to control supposedly involuntary body conditions such as pulse and temperature), and the preservation of the earth's environment.

Meanwhile, the practical results of her work have appeared in dozens of areas. Among the most useful of these is medicine: The realization that disease-causing bacteria gain resistance to antibiotics by "turning on" drug-resistance genes, then passing them to their offspring, has helped physicians find better ways to treat many infections. When doctors know how long it takes a certain bacteria to become resistant to penicillin, for instance, they can switch to another drug at just the right time, to kill the newly resistant generation of bacteria. Such knowledge has also alerted scientists to the problem that dosing animals raised for meat with antibiotics to speed their growth may cause resistant germs to evolve and flourish in the animals and perhaps also in the people who eat their meat.

Research has shown how some parasites, such as the one that causes African sleeping sickness, can actually change themselves through their genes so that the human immune system (the body system that fights off disease) will neither recognize them nor defend against them. The movable genetic elements McClintock found may even be involved in the way normal cells turn into cancerous ones; further study of this area could someday bring effective methods for preventing the disease.

For scientists who study better methods of growing crops, McClintock's work also continues to have important implications. Because growing sufficient food is one of the most important of human activities, federal grants for research on it since 1978 have grown faster than for any other scientific work according to the National Science Foundation. Workers in this area are manipulating genes of rice and corn in efforts to create plants that produce larger yields of more nutritious grain, resist insects and diseases, and grow with less water.

One such grain, called QPM (quality protein maize), is being tested by Richard Brissani of the Nutrition Institute of Central America and Panama. His investigations are concerned with determining whether young children can grow normally when weaned from their mother's milk to a formula made with QPM flour. If the children can, infants in parts of the world where food is scarce may have a better chance to survive. Preliminary results from Brissani's and other researchers' work are promising, and scientists from about 40 countries are already testing whether the corn will grow well in their climates.

McClintock's story is also important in the history of science itself, especially for women in science. When Barbara McClintock was growing up in the early 1900s, science was not considered a normal pursuit for a girl. By the 1980s, attitudes have changed, and women are not as likely to be discouraged from entering science careers or to face such obvious obstacles as McClintock did when they try to become scientists. In addition, since the enactment of the Civil Rights Act of 1964, discrimination against women is illegal; the plant-breeding department of a university today, for example, would not be able to deny admittance to a woman student solely because of her gender, as Cornell's plant-breeding department did to McClintock in the 1920s, or use gender as the basis for refusing to promote a young professor, as the University of Missouri did in McClintock's case in the 1930s. Better education and job opportunities in the 1980s have increased the number of women in many scientific fields; in engineering, for instance, there were 10 times more women in 1984 than in 1974, according to an article by Lilli Hornig in the November 1984 issue of *Technology Review*. Between 1976 and 1980, said Hornig, the proportion of computer scientists who were women rose from 13 percent to 30 percent.

Although the doors of science are still not as wide open to women as to men—differences in hiring, pay, and rates of promotion still exist, for example, and women in science who choose to marry and have families face difficult choices in balancing home and career responsibilities—the opportunities for young women entering careers in science today are vastly improved compared to the ones available in the early part of the century to McClintock. As top women scientists (such as Sally Ride and other women who work and have worked on NASA's space shuttle missions) become more numerous and better known, such opportunities will likely improve even more.

Barbara McClintock's greatest importance lies in her scientific work, however, not in her position as a role model or example. Her contributions to the world's knowledge of genetics, not the story of her career, are the central point of her life and work—as she would be the first to insist. Nevertheless, it is impossible not to be encouraged by McClintock's life, her work, and her attitude.

In her late eighties, Barbara McClintock is still working actively on her own research and remains excited about the future of science. Says science writer Barbara Shiels in her book on women Nobel Prize winners, although "in the year 2000 she [McClintock] will be ninety-eight, those who know her think she will probably be right there celebrating on that memorable New Year's Eve."

McClintock's own comment on what she expects from the future of

More nonscientists have come to know of McClintock's discoveries through the publicity her awards attracted. This 1989 exhibit at the Smithsonian Institution in Washington, D.C., included photographs of McClintock as a young woman at Cornell, at work in Cold Spring Harbor, and receiving the Nobel Prize. Above the pictures hang rows of multicolored ears of maize, examples of the organism that has fascinated McClintock for more than 50 years.

science is perhaps the most encouraging of all, however. This elderly, still-energetic woman who has spent her whole life in scientific research confided to Evelyn Fox Keller, "I can't wait. . . . I think it's going to be marvelous, simply marvelous."

McClintock enjoys a daily walk through the woods and fields of Cold Spring Harbor. She has always maintained that nature can tell researchers many things if only they will pay close attention and once said to her biographer: "If you'd only let the material tell you. . . . Organisms can do all types of things; they do fantastic things. They do everything we do and they do it better, more efficiently, more marvelously."

FURTHER READING

Calder, Nigel. *The Life Game: Evolution and the New Biology*. New York: Viking Press, 1973.

Dodd, Martha. *Through Embassy Eyes*. New York: Harcourt Brace & Co., 1939.

Judson, Horace Freeland. *The Eighth Day of Creation*. New York: Simon & Schuster, 1979.

Keller, Evelyn Fox. *A Feeling for the Organism: The Life and Work of Barbara McClintock*. New York: Freeman, 1984.

Kimball, John W. *Biology*. 5th ed. Reading, MA: Addison-Wesley, 1983.

Klein, Aaron E. *Threads of Life: Genetics From Aristotle to DNA*. New York: Natural History Press, 1970.

Margenau, Henry, and David Bergamini. *The Cell*. New York: Time Inc., 1964.

———. *The Scientist*. New York: Time Inc., 1964.

Shiels, Barbara. *Women and the Nobel Prize*. Minneapolis: Dillon Press, 1985.

CHRONOLOGY

June 16, 1902	Barbara McClintock born in Hartford, Connecticut
1908	McClintock family moves to Brooklyn, New York
1915	Barbara McClintock enters Erasmus Hall High School, Brooklyn
1919	Enrolls at Cornell University
1923	Earns B.A. in botany from Cornell
1925	Earns M.A. from Cornell; becomes the first to distinguish the 10 chromosomes in corn
1927	Receives Ph.D. in botany from Cornell University
1931	Publishes paper with Harriet Creighton and becomes the first to prove crossing-over in chromosomes exists; awarded two-year National Research Council Fellowship
1932	Honored for presentation at Sixth International Congress of Genetics
1933	Travels to Germany on Guggenheim grant
1936–41	Works as assistant professor of genetics at the University of Missouri
1942	Accepts appointment to research staff at Cold Spring Harbor, New York, funded by the Carnegie Institution of Washington
1944	Elected member of the National Academy of Sciences; investigates *Neurospora* chromosomes
1946–51	Discovers transposable genetic controlling elements in corn
1951	Cold Spring Harbor Symposium presentation of "transposition" fails
1954	Watson and Crick discover structure of DNA; McClintock appointed visiting professor at California Institute of Technology
1961	Monod and Jacob publish work similar to McClintock's
1963–69	McClintock works as consultant to the Agricultural Science Program of the Rockefeller Foundation
1965	Named Andrew D. White Professor-at-Large, Cornell University
1967	Receives National Academy of Sciences' Kimber Genetics Award
1970	Receives National Medal of Science
1972	Awarded honorary doctorate from Williams College
1979	Awarded honorary doctorates from Rockefeller University and Harvard University
1981	Receives Albert Lasker Basic Medical Research award; named MacArthur Prize Fellow Laureate; wins Wolf Prize in Medicine
1982	Awarded honorary doctorates from Yale University and the University of Cambridge, England; begins working with Steven Dellaporta at Cold Spring Harbor
1983	Receives Nobel Prize in medicine or physiology
1985	Becomes honorary member of the Medical Women's International Association, the New York Academy of Sciences, and the American Society of Naturalists; named honorary vice-president for the 16th International Congress of Genetics
1986	Wins National Women's Hall of Fame Award

INDEX

Mary Kittredge, former associate editor of the medical journal *Respiratory Care,* is now a free-lance writer of nonfiction. She is the author of *The Respiratory System* and *Prescription and Over-the-Counter Drugs* in the Chelsea House ENCYCLOPEDIA OF HEALTH series and has written a number of Chelsea House young-adult biographies, including *Marc Antony, Frederick the Great, Jane Addams,* and *Helen Hayes.* Her writing awards include the Ruell Crompton Tuttle Essay Prize and the Mystery Writers of America Robert L. Fish Award for best first short-mystery fiction of 1986. Ms. Kittredge received a B.A. from Trinity College in Hartford, Connecticut, and studied at the University of California Medical Center in San Francisco. Certified as a respiratory care technician by the American Association for Respiratory Therapy, she has been a member of the respiratory care staff at Yale–New Haven Hospital and Medical Center since 1972.

Matina S. Horner is president of Radcliffe College and associate professor of psychology and social relations at Harvard University. She is best known for her studies of women's motivation, achievement, and personality development. Dr. Horner serves on several national boards and advisory councils, including those of the National Science Foundation, Time Inc., and the Women's Research and Education Institute. She earned her B.A. from Bryn Mawr College and Ph.D. from the University of Michigan, and holds honorary degrees from many colleges and universities, including Mount Holyoke, Smith, Tufts, and the University of Pennsylvania.